Ronald Reagan, President

RONALD REAGAN, PRESIDENT

by John Devaney

Walker and Company
New York

For Domenico Masciocchi

First published in the United States of America in 1990 by Walker Publishing Company, Inc.

Published simultaneously in Canada by Thomas Allen & Son Canada, Limited, Markham, Ontario

Library of Congress Cataloging-in-Publication Data
Devaney, John.
    Ronald Reagan, president / by John Devaney.
      p. cm.
    Summary: A biography of the fortieth president of the United States.
    ISBN 0-8027-6931-4.—ISBN 0-8027-6932-2 (lib. bdg.)
    1. Reagan, Ronald—Juvenile literature. 2. Presidents—United States—Biography—Juvenile literature. [1. Reagan, Ronald.
2. Presidents.] I. Title.
E877.D47   1990
973.927'092—dc20
[B]
[92]   90-31102
                                         CIP
                                       AC

Printed in the United States of America

2 4 6 8 10 9 7 5 3 1

Contents

The Lifeguard

The drowning swimmer strained to raise his arm, hoping to catch the attention of the lifeguard on the shore. But the man's hand poked upward only inches above the rushing white water of Rock River.

On the shore the tall, lanky lifeguard sat high on his stand. A teenage girl came by and pointed at a log.

"How many you got now, Dutch?"

"Don't know," the nineteen-year-old lifeguard said with a smile. "You count 'em."

She looked down at the log, counting the notches that had been cut into it. There were more than sixty. Each notch stood for one drowning swimmer Dutch Reagan had pulled from Rock River. During a summer three years earlier, four swimmers had drowned in the fast-flowing river. During the past three years, ever since Dutch Reagan had become lifeguard, not one person had drowned.

Dutch liked being a lifeguard. No one in the town of Dixon, Illinois, could swim faster than Dutch. He had smashed all of his high school's swimming record.

"Being a lifeguard is fun," Dutch told his friends.

Fun? They rolled their eyes. Diving into the roaring Rock River to wrestle 200-pound grown ups to safety didn't seem like fun to them. It seemed positively dangerous.

1

This photo of Rock River's lifeguard was taken by a girl friend of Mugs'. Only once did Dutch ever get a reward. A swimmer hit the water too hard and lost his false teeth. Dutch dived into the river, found the false teeth—and got a ten dollar finder's fee.
COURTESY REAGAN PRESIDENTIAL MATERIALS STAFF

"You know why I had such fun at it?" Dutch later said. "Because I was the only one up there on the guardstand. It was like a stage. Everyone had to look at me."

The fifteen-year-old girl stared up at Dutch, awe in her eyes after looking at all those notches.

Suddenly Dutch shot upward from his chair. He saw the man's head bobbing weakly some hundred yards out in the churning river.

Dutch leaped off the stand, raced to the river's bank, dived into the white water. A woman screamed, seeing her husband thrashing helplessly. The lifeguard seemed too far away. The hundreds of bathers stood rigid, watching silently under the pale blue summer sky.

Dutch churned like a speedboat toward the flailing man. The man's head sank below the water, then bobbed to the tossing surface.

"Got you!" Dutch shouted, grabbing the man's arm. "Relax, we'll make it!"

Minutes later, the six-foot, 175-pound Dutch carried the man ashore in his arms. "Oh, I could have made it all right," the man gasped to his wife. People snickered, knowing the man didn't like being saved by a teenager half his age.

Dutch walked back to his stand. A boy was cutting another notch in the log. Dutch smiled. His father, Jack, would be proud. It had been Jack's idea to cut the notches in the log.

Dutch saw Margaret Cleaver coming toward the stand with other friends from Dixon Northside High. He heard their shouts, cheering him for the rescue. Dutch adored "Mugs," as he called Margaret. In school plays she was often the leading lady, Dutch the leading man. The two were now "going steady," as teenagers said in the 1930s, dating no one else.

Dutch liked to write. He had written a high school essay about being a lifeguard and how no one ever thanked lifeguards for saving their lives. But, he had written, there was one person who made lifeguarding worthwhile:

". . . she's walking onto the dock now. . . . The lifeguard strolls by . . . She speaks and the sound of her voice is like balm to a wounded soul . . ."

Dutch often created make-believe scenes like that in his mind. As long as he could remember, he had written plays or daydreamed about moments when he ran 100 yards to score his football team's winning touchdown, or how he had saved someone from Rock River and won a thousand-dollar reward. "I lived in a world of pretend," he once said about growing up.

His world of pretend, however, was fast coming to an end. Dutch would soon enter a real world where men, women, and children fought over pails of garbage so they could eat. This was the grey, cold, harsh world of The Great Depression. This was a world where long lines of men and women, and even children, begged for jobs—and doors slammed shut in their faces. This was a world where frightened children watched as their fathers and mothers carried belongings out of their homes, thrown out because they could not pay the rent.

Dutch Reagan would soon enter that world of "bad times," as Americans called the Depression of the 1930s. What he would find in the real world would be triumphs many times greater than any he could have imagined in his world of pretend.

The Football Player

The blizzard ripped through the tiny town of Tampico, Illinois (population 1,276), all during the night and early into the morning of February 6, 1911. In a room above a bakery on Main Street, a new-born baby let out his first screech. The baby's father looked down at the squalling baby and said, "For such a little bit of a Dutchman, he makes a lot of noise, doesn't he?"

Jack Reagan, a shoe salesman, bragged loudly about his "fat little baby," whom he thought looked like a Dutchman. The baby's mother, Nelle Wilson Reagan, named the baby Ronald Wilson Reagan. But Ronald Reagan—to those who knew him as a boy—would always be called "Dutch."

Jack Reagan (he pronounced it Ray-gun, not Ree-gun) had grown up in the midwest, the grandson of Irish-Catholic immigrants. Dark and handsome, with an athlete's muscular build, he dressed nattily, shoes polished, a cocky smile brightening his salesman's face. Jack was a dreamer. He dreamed that one day he would own a shoe empire.

But Jack worked mostly in small towns, where families wore hand-me-down shoes. A boy would wear shoes worn ten years earlier by his big brothers. Jack worked long hours, but he shuffled from one low-paying shoe selling job to the next.

Jack drank whiskey to make him forget how impossible was his dream. When he got his week's pay, Jack threw the money

5

across tavern bars as he gulped down glasses of brain-numbing alcohol. He stumbled home, collapsing on the floor. His wife Nelle found his empty wallet—and stared at stacks of unpaid grocery bills.

Her two babies cried hungrily in their cribs. Dutch's older brother, Neil, had been born three years before Dutch. Neil had been nicknamed Moon, the name of a character in a newspaper comic strip.

Jack decided he might make his dream come true in the big city. Early in 1914 he and Nelle, three-year-old Dutch and six-year-old Moon moved to Chicago. Jack sold shoes in a downtown department store. The family lived on the south side of Chicago in a cramped, gas-lit apartment that had no heat or hot water.

Jack still threw his money to bartenders and tossed back shots of whiskey. Nelle often had no more than a dime to buy food. A dime would buy a soupbone. Moon brought home the soupbone after he'd asked the butcher for a free sliver of liver for his cat. Since there was no Reagan cat, liver became the Reagan's Sunday feast. Nelle used the soupbone to boil a brimming pot of soup. She tossed in scraps of potatoes and carrots, plus cups of water—lots of water. The soup had to last a week until Jack's next payday.

The Chicago store fired Jack for drinking. The family moved westward to Galesburg, Illinois, where a relative helped Jack find work in a cheap shoe store.

If Jack was a dreamer, Nelle was a doer. Her grandparents had sailed from Scotland to pan for gold in California. She grew up as a Protestant and became a member of the Christian (or Disciples of Christ) Church. Moon had been baptized a Catholic, like his father. But Nelle had insisted that Dutch be baptized a member of the Protestant Christian Church. Moon remained a Catholic all his life, Dutch a Protestant.

Small, with piercing blue eyes and reddish-brown hair, Nelle read her New Testament every day. She taught children at Sunday School. She visited sick children and prayed for them to get well. The town's mothers believed Nelle could heal the sick with a touch and a prayer.

Jack and Nelle and their two children, Moon (left) and Dutch. This photo was taken in Tampico when Dutch was two-years-old. During one Christmas there, the boys wanted an electric train. Nelle said the family couldn't afford it—but Jack and she surprised them with the train.
COURTESY REAGAN PRESIDENTIAL MATERIALS STAFF

Nelle lived by Jesus' teaching: "What you do for the least among you, you do for Me." The "least" included men and women in jail. Nelle visited them, bringing food and her smiling, perky cheer. When convicts were let out of the Tampico jail and had no place to live, Nelle invited them to live in a spare room of the Reagans' small apartment. She shared the small amount of food in her cupboard with the jailed, the sick, the poor. In his autobiography, "Where's the Rest of Me?' Dutch wrote of his mother, "She was a practical do-gooder."

At a Sunday School class one day, Nelle called divorce a sin. Later she learned that one child in the class had parents who were divorced. Nelle threw herself at the child's knees. She begged forgiveness for embarrassing the child. A neighbor once said, "That was Nelle."

Neighbors brought food for the babies while Jack slept off his drunken stupors. Women told Nelle to leave Jack. "No," she told them, "somehow the Lord will provide."

Five-year-old Dutch often sat near his mother to follow her fingers as she read words to him from a book. Dutch stretched out on the floor one evening, trying to read a newspaper. "Suddenly," he recalled later in his life story, "all the funny black marks on the paper clicked into place."

His father came into the room and asked what he was doing.

"Reading," Dutch said.

Jack stared. The boy was too young to be able to read. "Well, read me something," Jack snapped.

Dutch began to read a news story about a bombing in San Francisco. Nelle overheard and rushed into the room. She called to neighbors and stood, pride in her eyes, as her Dutch showed everyone that he could read.

In his first-grade classroom Dutch peered at the blackboard. What he saw were blurred white-on-black lines. "I thought," he wrote in his autobiography, "that the whole world was made up of colored blobs that became distinct when I got closer." He assumed everyone saw only colored blobs.

Yet he got good grades in school. He could open a book, glance at a page, and names and dates stuck to his memory. He could memorize quickly anything he read.

This 1917 photo shows the first grade class at Tampico's one-room schoolhouse. The future President of the United States holds his left hand to his mouth at the far left of the second row. Dutch lived with his parents in a five room flat that had no indoor toilet. The rooms were heated during frigid midwestern winters by a single coal-burning stove. Windows overlooked an alley.
COURTESY PRESIDENTIAL MATERIALS STAFF

Moon seemed more like his father—loud, fun-loving, always on the go. Strong and athletic, Moon ran with mischief-making gangs. Moon sneered at scrawny Dutch and called him a sissy.

Like Nelle (the boys called Jack and Nelle by their first names), Dutch could read for hours, stretched on the floor, nose in the pages of a book. Nelle read plays. She would play the role of a heroine in a Greek tragedy. She read the lines to an adoring audience of one—her son Dutch.

Each Saturday the seven-year-old Dutch got a few pennies from his mother. He scampered to the "nickelodian," as movie houses were then called. He and his pals watched the silent movies of the day. The boys and girls laughed at The Little Tramp, Charlie Chaplin. Dutch idolized Tom Mix, a handsome cowboy who drew fast and shot straight.

In 1916 the United States joined England and France in World War I against Germany and its allies. Jack wanted to go to France to fight "The Huns," as he called the Germans. But he was too old to be a soldier. Jack strode off to his taverns—another dream smashed that he had to forget in an alcoholic mist.

Late in 1918 the war ended, Germany defeated. Ten-year-old Moon and seven-year-old Dutch stood on the sidewalk to cheer the marching soldiers coming home from France. Jack again had been fired for drinking. The family had shuffled off to another small town. The Reagans now lived in Monmouth, a few miles west of Galesburg.

Dutch entered the third grade in Monmouth. His teacher stared, surprised, as the new boy quickly memorized multiplication and division tables. Years later a Monmouth schoolmate told Anne Edwards, the author of "Young Reagan": "He had super ability, and—I guess—class."

Americans had never been richer. The guns, ships, and bombs turned out by America's factories had smashed Germany. Those factories paid high salaries to workers during the war. Salaries for other workers soared—but so did prices.

Jack's salary stayed low. Illinois farmers still did not buy a lot of shoes. Jack went on dreaming that he could suddenly get rich. He bought for a cheap price a shipment of rotting potatoes. He ordered Moon and Dutch to sit in a freight car and sort the good potatoes from the bad.

The boys sweltered in the freight car under a blazing summer sun. The rotting potatoes began to stink in the humid air of the freight car. They let out an odor, Dutch later recalled, "worse than that of a decaying corpse."

For week after week Moon and Dutch retched in that stinking freight car. One morning they told each other: Enough is enough. They tossed most of the potatoes into a dump. It was a long time before Dutch ate another potato.

In 1919 Jack took a job managing a shoe store in Tampico,

back where Dutch had been born. Returning to Tampico after five years, Dutch—now eight years old—quickly made friends with boys like Monkey Welch. Dutch, Monkey and other boys rode on their bikes to a nearby canal, its water deep and swift. The boys raced each other as they swam across the canal—and Dutch always won. Even tall and husky twelve year olds churned, panting, in Dutch's wake.

"You could be an Olympic swimmer some day," Monkey told Dutch. Dutch shook his head. Ever since a few months earlier, Dutch Reagan knew what he wanted to be more than anything else in the world. He wanted to be an All-American football hero, the hero who took the ball and ran 100 yards for the winning touchdown.

The mob of boys, all nine or ten years old, formed a ragged line across the vacant lot. On the opposite side of the lot stood another mob of boys, who also formed a wavy line. In the middle of this line crouched the smallest boy of the two groups—nine-year-old Dutch Reagan. He stood only four-foot-eight, weighing about ninety pounds. A grin split his thin face—he was about to play his first game of football.

A boy in Dutch's line ran forward and kicked the lumpy ball. It soared through the air. A boy in the other line ran forward and caught it. Screaming shrilly, the two lines of boys charged at each other.

Dutch led his line's charge. "I got a wild exhilaration," he once said, "out of jumping first into a pile-up."

Dozens of boys piled on top of Dutch, who sank like a stone to the bottom of the heap. He saw only darkness and squirming bodies. He began to tremble, fearing he would be suffocated.

When the boys untangled, the pint-sized Dutch leaped to his feet and his fear vanished. He wanted to charge down the field again—and he did—as one mob kicked off to the other. This, to boys in a dusty Illinois village in 1920, was all they knew about football. The boys had never seen a real game.

"I worshipped the wild charge down the field," Dutch later remembered in his first autobiography, "Where's the Rest of Me?" He grinned devilishly as he bowled over bigger boys and saw the stunned looks on their faces. That was proving you could grow up to be a man and become what Dutch daydreamed he might be one day—a hero.

But nine-year-old Dutch wasn't built for football—nor for most other sports. When kids chose sides for games, they picked Dutch last. Dutch lunged to tackle runners and missed by yards. In baseball he swung at pitches over his head. The pitch seemed to jump out of a blur and shoot past him. To Dutch, any object more than two yards away looked blurry. He thought things two yards away looked blurry to everyone. Dutch and his parents did not know that he was near-sighted.

One evening Dutch and Monkey listened, almost breathless, to a neighbor's "crystal set," as the first radios were called. Earphones clamped to his head, Dutch heard a scratchy, faraway announcer's voice: "This is KDKA, Pittsburgh . . ."

The two boys and about twenty grownups listened until the station went off the air. Then Dutch leaped up and imitated perfectly the scratchy voice: "This is KDKA, Pittsburgh . . . KDKA, Pittsburgh."

Monkey and the grownups laughed and applauded. Ronald Reagan had heard for the first time what keeps actors coming back for bows—the warming sound of applause.

Dutch liked to go with his mother when she entertained the ladies club of Tampico by reading parts from popular melodramas such as *East Lynne*. Nelle read the lines in tragic tones, often weeping as she read. Dutch stared, fascinated by how make-believe seemed so real.

Late in 1920 Jack got an offer to become part owner of The Fashion Boot Shop, which sold expensive shoes, in nearby Dixon, Illinois, some ninety miles west of Chicago. Jack bought a used car. It was the first car he had ever owned. The Reagans packed all their belongings onto the car's roof. Crammed into the car, Moon and Dutch waved goodbye to their Tampico pals. Billowing dust behind them, the Reagans roared off to Dixon, the place that would forever be Dutch Reagan's home town.

"All of us have a place to go back to," Ronald Reagan once said. "Dixon is that place for me. This was the place that shaped my body and mind for all the years to come."

The Scrub

"Can we have a dime to go to the movies, Jack?"

The thirteen-year-old Moon looked up at his father, hand held out. Ten-year-old Dutch, his arms as thin as sticks, also held out a hand. A new silent movie had come to the nickelodeon in Dixon.

"What do you think, that I'm made of money?" Jack growled.

"Ah, please," Moon begged. "Every kid in town is going to see this new movie, *Birth of a Nation*."

"*Birth of a Nation!*" Jack shouted. "That's the movie that favors the Ku Klux Klan!"

Ku Klux Klan members wore white hoods. They rode at night to torture and hang blacks for the "crime" of thinking they were the equal of whites. The Klan preached hatred for blacks, Catholics and Jews. In *Birth of a Nation*, Ku Klux Klansmen were portrayed as heroes.

No Reagan would see that movie, Jack said. The Klan was evil.

Disliking someone because he or she was different, Jack believed, was wrong. Once, while on a trip, he stopped at a hotel. When he signed his name to the register, the clerk said, "You'll be glad to know, Mr. Reagan, that we're happy to have Irish people here but we don't take in Jews."

Jack threw down the pen. "If you don't take Jews," he said, "you soon won't be taking Irish." He slept in his frigid car and

13

Thirteen-year-old Dutch stands on the front lawn of his home on South Hennepin Avenue in Dixon. He is wearing the knee-length knickers then popular among pre-high school boys.
COURTESY REAGAN PRESIDENTIAL MATERIALS STAFF

caught a cold. A week later he had a heart attack. It was the first of several that would later kill him.

By now, 1922, Americans faced what they called "hard times." Factories shut their doors as the wartime need for machines and other products fell. Many people no longer had jobs—nor the money to buy things. Farmers got lower prices for their corn and wheat. They had fewer dollars in their pockets to buy shoes at Jack's Fashion Boot Shop. Stores in Dixon needed those dollars from farmers to stay open. The town of 10,000 sat amid hundreds of Illinois farms.

Jack worked long hours at the store. He told the boys that money would soon start to flow into the shoe store. He had always been a Democrat. He stayed a Democrat, even though most of his customers in Dixon were Republicans.

"All we need," Jack told Dutch and Moon, "is for the Democrats to take charge of the country." A Republican, Calvin Coolidge, was now President (Warren Harding had died in office). In 1924, Jack predicted, the Democrats would defeat Coolidge.

When the Reagans had first come to Dixon in 1920, they lived in a big house with four bedrooms. But Jack could no longer afford the rent. They moved to a much smaller house. Dutch and Moon shivered as they slept on a drafty enclosed porch. Nelle earned a few dollars a week sewing for neighbors. She told Jack that the Lord would provide. "We were poor," Dutch later said, "but we didn't know we were poor." Everyone else in Dixon was just as poor.

Jack told his sons that hard work would make anybody a success. "Man's own ambition," he told Dutch, "determines what happens to him the rest of his life."

As a boy, Jack had heard stories from his parents of pioneer days in the west. When a man in those days needed food for his family, he had to know how to hunt or his family starved to death. When a baby got sick, a woman had to know how to care for it, or the baby died. When Indians attacked, men and women had to know how to shoot straight, or they died horribly. The government's cavalry charge over the hill to rescue pioneers, Jack told Dutch, happened only in the movies. In real-life 19th century America, Jack said, men and women had to rely on themselves—not on the government.

Dutch saw how his mother helped the poor and the sick. His mother believed, Dutch once said, "that everyone loved her because she loved them." It was right, Dutch grew up believing, that neighbors help each other in bad times. But asking for help from the town, county or state—"going on the dole," as they sneered in Dixon—was only for those too old or too sick to work.

Dutch grew up sharing his parents' belief that hard work and God's help would pull people upward to success. No healthy, self-respecting person, Dutch and his father believed, went on the government's dole.

Some ten years later, both his father and Dutch would have that belief put to a very tough test.

To the scrawny Dutch, growing up in Dixon was "a Tom Sawyer-boyhood." He fished in Rock River. He ran through the woods, playing cowboys and Indians. He imagined riding a horse across the flat countryside like his hero Tom Mix. One day when he was rich, he told himself, he would own a horse.

His favorite pastime was playing football on dusty lots. He imagined he was All-America Red Grange, the Galloping Ghost of the University of Illinois' Fighting Illini. The twelve-year-old Dutch stood only five feet tall and weighed barely a hundred pounds. But he daydreamed that he stood six feet and weighed a brawny two-hundred pounds. Watching a western movie or reading an adventure or sports book—he read at least two a week—he imagined he was the hero who defeats the villains or scores the last-second touchdown.

After school he and a pal, Ed O'Malley, played two-on-two football games against Ed's big brother, George, and Moon—the "kids" against the "older guys."

Dutch always wanted to carry the ball. He charged at the older boys, seeing only blurs. Moon or George stuck out a leg and tripped the charging Dutch. He flew through the air and skidded across the ground. The boys laughed. Dutch bounced up, bruises on his thin face, and begged to carry the ball again.

Dutch took swimming lessons at the Dixon YMCA. "Dutch could swim, as quick as an eel," a friend said. For the first time, Dutch won in sports. He shot ahead of sixteen year olds in YMCA races. "You'll be a champion swimmer," other boys said.

The skinny Dutch shrugged. Who wanted to be a champion swimmer? He wanted to be an All-American football player.

His mother took Dutch to Sunday school and to Bible classes each Sunday evening. At the Bible classes, the teacher asked the children to read passages in the New Testament. Dutch had learned, from listening to his mother, how to read with dramatic emphasis. When she read lines, she suddenly raised or lowered her voice. That trick, he noticed, kept her listeners on the edge of their seats.

"Dutch would lower his voice almost to a whisper, then suddenly lift it to a shout," a friend once recalled. "He gave the readings an extra something. He made the Bible stories sound as if they had all happened yesterday. And there was always that special boyish smile of his, those blue-gray eyes looking straight at you."

Dutch sat in the front row of his eighth grade class in Dixon, barely able to make out the writing on the blackboard. But teachers never guessed he saw only blurs. His grades were always B's and A's. Dutch would read, close the book, and then recite every name and date he had just read.

One spring morning in 1924, Jack took the family for a Sunday drive. Thirteen-year-old Dutch sat in the back of the car with Moon. Dutch listened, proud but also with envy, as Moon told how he had scored a touchdown for his high school's football team the previous fall. The stocky, speedy Moon ran away from defenders to catch long passes.

Dutch imagined himself catching a long pass for a touchdown. But Dutch knew he couldn't see a ball clearly if it were more than two feet away from him.

"Look at that sign," Moon suddenly said, pointing to an advertising billboard. "Isn't that funny—what the sign says?"

Dutch stared at the sign. He saw only blurred words. He was angry that he couldn't see what had made Moon laugh. He leaned forward and snatched the eyeglasses off his mother, who was also near-sighted. Dutch snapped on her spectacles.

"I was astounded," he later wrote in his autobiography, *Where's The Rest of Me?* The entire world around him had suddenly snapped into sharp focus. He could see clearly the words on the sign. He looked at trees and saw the sharp lines of their leaves. He saw hills etched starkly against the sky. For all of his life, he had looked at the world through murky waters. Now the water had suddenly turned crystal clear.

His mother bought him dark, horn-rimmed glasses. Dutch could read the words on blackboards. But he knew he couldn't wear glasses amid the flying elbows of football games (contact lenses had not yet been invented).

"You won't have to worry about how to see in football games," Moon said, laughing. "You're too small and skinny to play high school football."

That fall of 1924, thirteen-year-old Dutch walked through the doors of Dixon Northside High as a freshman. He stood five foot three and weighed one hundred and five pounds. "The football team," a coach told him, "doesn't have pants small enough to fit you."

But he'd make the team, Dutch told himself. One day, like Moon, he would wear the purple and white Dixon jersey. He'd start by playing for the scrub team. The scrubs were beaten black and blue during the week by the varsity as "the big team" practiced for Saturday's game.

Each afternoon Dutch walked home from practice bruised and bloodied. He was usually grinning.

"I knew," he said years later, "I'd grow up someday. And I was learning the fundamentals of football."

Today he had learned how to slither off blockers to tackle a runner. Tomorrow, he'd work hard to learn how to slip a block even faster. He'd work as hard as he could to earn the purple and white. And maybe—he was certainly praying hard enough—the Lord might help.

The Actor

"You're pretty young to be a lifeguard," the woman said. She glanced at the lean, fifteen-year-old Dutch Reagan, who stood side by side with his father on a spring day in 1926.

The year before, Dutch had soared to a sinewy 5-foot-9, 145 pounds. He had broken most of the swimming records at Northside High. In the spring of 1926, several people had drowned in the Rock River, which rushed deep and fast through Dixon's Lowell Park recreation area. The town officials talked about closing the park. Dutch told Mrs. Ruth Graybill, who supervised the park, that a lifeguard could save people from drowning and the park could stay open.

"He can do it," Jack said to Mrs. Graybill. "Give him a chance."

Dutch was hired. He worked from ten in the morning until ten at night, seven days a week. He got $18 a week—and all the five-cent root beers and ten-cent hamburgers he could eat.

"He liked the job and we liked him," Ruth Graybill told Reagan biographer Anne Edwards years later. "In the mornings, if he had time, he would give small children swimming lessons. He was a wonderful, good-natured young man. I never heard him speak one cross word to the bathers. He was a beautiful diver. He would do the swan dive out on the spring board."

19

"He was the perfect specimen of an athlete," a pal remembers. "He was tall, willowy, muscular, brown, good-looking, and of course, the girls were always flocking around him."

In that first summer as a lifeguard, Dutch saved more than a dozen swimmers from drowning. Jack had told him to cut a notch in an old log for each life he saved. When asked how many notches were on the log, Dutch always said, "I don't know, you count 'em." But he knew exactly how many notches were on that log—seventy seven after six summers as the Lowell Park lifeguard. And in that time not one person drowned in Rock River.

Attending Christian Church services with his mother, Dutch had noticed Margaret Cleaver, the pert, sparkling, pretty daughter of the minister. He stared at her more often than he looked at his New Testament. When Dutch became a lifeguard, Margaret began to look at him, standing tall on the lifeguard's stand.

With as many as a hundred swimmers in the river, Dutch had little chance to talk to Margaret, or Mugs as he called her. But late in the evenings, when only a few people were still swimming, Dutch sometimes picked up a pebble and skittered it across the water. Startled bathers looked to Dutch, who would say, "Oh, that's just an old river rat." That got everyone out of the river. Then Dutch might borrow a friend's canoe and with Mugs facing him, paddle the canoe down the river, his small hand-cranked phonograph playing their favorite song, Ramona.

"Me—I was in love . . ." Dutch later wrote. Mugs told him they were too young to be anything but good friends. But after a while they dated only each other.

Dutch wore his new horn-rimmed glasses to read blackboards during classes. But he disliked the way he looked in spectacles. He wore them only when he had to see something far away. He rarely studied the night before a test. He could open a book half an hour before a test, read a page for the first time—and get an A. But Dutch didn't push to get A's. "I worked hard to get passing grades in school," he once said, "because if you got below C, you weren't allowed to play football."

In his junior year, the fall of 1927, the "new Dutch," bigger and stronger, made the varsity as a second-string guard. Now five foot ten and one hundred sixty pounds, Dutch used the skills he had learned as a scrub, plus his wild-eyed enthusiasm, to bowl over bigger ball carriers. "Trouble was," a teammate once said, "Dutch's eyesight was so bad he sometimes tackled a guy who didn't have the ball."

Late in the 1927 season the coach thought his first-string guard had become lazy. Just before a big game, he assembled the team in the dressing room and called out his starting lineup. "At right guard," he said slowly, "Reagan, you're starting."

"I can never describe," Dutch later wrote, "how I felt."

Dutch kept that starting job—and won his purple and white Dixon jersey. "I could only see a yard and a half," he once said, "but nobody within a yard and a half got by me."

"I never had a player," his coach said, "who tried harder or who had more enthusiasm than Dutch." The lazy guard never got back the starting job.

Dutch went to high school during the middle part of the decade known as The Roaring Twenties. Bad times had turned to good times. Millions around the globe demanded American cars, American movies, American steel. "Made in the U.S.A." meant the best.

Skyscrapers climbed higher and higher in American cities. Trains zipped coast to coast and now you could fly New York to Los Angeles in under twelve hours.

Factories belched fire and smoke from their smokestacks day and night. Workers pocketed fat paychecks. They bought products unknown to most Americans ten years earlier: refrigerators, electric washing machines, telephones, radios. They bought whiskey even though the sale of liquor was against the law, banned by an amendment to the constitution called Prohibition. Gangsters sold whiskey in places called speakeasys and bribed cops to look the other way.

On Wall Street in New York, the stock market soared upward. The prices of shares of stock in American companies had never been higher. Men and women bought stocks of companies like General Motors at $10 a share. They watched the price shoot upward to $100 a share—and even higher. Some people worried, saying, "Those shares are not worth half that price." But millions of others rushed to buy stocks. Everyone, it seemed, could become rich almost overnight.

Except the farmers. American farmers had to charge more for their beef, vegetables and fruit than farmers in South America, for example. The reason: Farmers in the United States had to pay more for labor and machinery. American farmers were spending more money than they took in. Some went broke and had to sell their farms.

Farmers around Dixon now had fewer dollars to buy luxuries like an extra pair of shoes. Dutch himself wore Moon's old shoes all through high school. Jack worked hard, long hours. He studied books on how to sell more shoes. With his Irish eyes smiling, he told jokes to customers. "I'm glad you chose that pair. They can walk you to church and dance a jig on the way home."

But Jack now recognized the truth: he would never be a shoe tycoon. More than ever, he numbed the hurts inside himself with long pulls from a whisky bottle. One day Dutch came home from school to see his father stretched unconscious on the porch.

"He was drunk, dead to the world," Dutch wrote in *Where's the Rest of Me?* "I bent over him, smelling the sharp odor from the speakeasy. I got a fistful of his overcoat. Opening the door, I managed to drag him inside and get him to bed."

Nelle told Dutch that Jack had a sickness, what Jack himself called "a weakness" and "the black curse." "We must help him and love him," she told Dutch.

Dutch knew that Jack's drinking drained money from the family. Nelle still took in sewing and now worked part time at a Dixon store as a clerk. Neighbors sent food. Liver "for the cat" was still the big Sunday meal. Years later, Washington Post writer Lou Cannon asked Reagan, then the Governor of California, about his parents. He talked for fifteen minutes about his mother. He never mentioned his father.

But like Jack, Dutch was a Democrat. He told his friends he could hardly wait until he was twenty-one so he could vote. In 1924, the Republicans had again won the Presidency, the country re-electing Calvin Coolidge. The President said that what was good for big business and Wall Street would be good for little businessmen like farmers.

Farm prices, however, continued to slide. "In 1928," Jack told Dutch and Moon, "that Governor of New York, Al Smith, will be elected President." At the 1924 Democratic nominating convention, one speaker had hailed Al Smith as The Happy Warrior who could win the Presidency. The speaker had to be lifted onto the platform to speak because a disease called infantile paralysis had withered the muscles of his legs. Many Democrats hoped that one day Franklin Delano Roosevelt might run for President.

Dutch still liked to write plays in his mind, acting out the roles as he walked down the street. Grown-ups stared at the boy who was always talking to himself.

He began to write poems for the *Dixonian*, the school's literary magazine. One, titled "Life," opened with these four lines:

> I wonder what it's all about, and why
> We suffer so when little things go wrong?
> We make our life a struggle,
> When life should be a song.

Life was no song to his father. Life for Jack had been a struggle against bad luck and his "weakness." But Jack Reagan had raised a son who looked at bad times as the chance to turn them into good times. Dutch was growing up an optimist. A *Washington Post* reporter, Dan Balz, grew up near Dixon. Growing up in the 1920's in a small town like Dixon, Balz says, "leaves you with the feeling that people are basically good and will treat you right. Ronald Reagan exudes that."

One of Dutch's English teachers, B.J. Fraser, asked Dutch to join the school's Dramatic Club. Dutch joined eagerly, one reason being that the pretty Mugs was a member. Mugs nearly always won the role of a play's leading lady.

"Why, why are the characters doing these things?" Fraser asked his students. He told them to act like the character they were playing by asking, as they read a script: "Why am I reading these lines?"

Years later an actor named Marlon Brando and an actress named Marilyn Monroe would make popular this kind of "Method" acting. Dutch thought that was the only way to act. "When he got on stage," Fraser once said, "he was the character."

When his football teammates kidded Dutch about becoming "a sissy actor," Dutch laughed and said, "I just go to the rehearsals because then I get to walk home with the leading lady."

"Dutch," Fraser later said, "stood head and shoulders above the other members of the Dramatic Club." Soon Dutch played the dashing leading man to Mugs' leading lady in comedies like *You and I.* He could also be a menacing pirate in tense melodramas like *Captain Applejack.*

"He fit into almost any kind of role you put him into," B.J. Fraser often said. In one play Dutch played the fast-talking reporter whose wisecracks drew roaring laughter from the audience. In another play he became a starry-eyed, romantic poet—and girls in the audience sighed.

Dutch told Fraser that he hoped to go to college, become an All-American football player, and then earn lots of money in pro football, as Red Grange was doing. But if football didn't work out, Dutch asked, did Mr. Fraser think he could make a living as an actor?

Few American actors made much money, Fraser told him. The exceptions, he said, were one in a thousand, a handful who became millionaires making silent movies in Hollywood.

Dutch didn't talk about becoming an actor to anyone else. In a small town like Dixon in the 1920s, wanting to become an actor was like wanting to become a painter or a poet.

He knew he wanted to go to college. Specifically Eureka College in nearby Eureka, Illinois. It was a Christian college, Mugs would be going there, and it had a football team, the Golden Cyclones, whose star a few years earlier had been what sportswriters called "a triple threat." A triple threat could run, pass and kick. The Cyclone's triple threat was Garland Waggoner who came from Dutch's hometown of Dixon and was one of Dutch's biggest idols.

Dutch had saved $400 from his lifeguard pay. That was all the money he had. His mother and father could give him nothing. Tuition at Eureka cost $180 a year. His room and board would cost at least $400. He didn't have enough money even for one year at Eureka, never mind for the four years he needed to graduate.

But on a hot September morning in 1928, Dutch threw his bags into the rumbleseat of Mugs' small car. They drove toward Eureka. Dutch told himself he would find a way to pay for his four years at Eureka. He had found a way to win the purple and white jersey at Northside High, hadn't he? Luck—the laziness of a starting guard had helped—but so had hard work as a scrub and lots of prayer. Dutch Reagan carried a willingness to work as well as to pray with him to Eureka. And waiting in that small town was a once-in-a-lifetime stroke of luck. This time luck would have nothing to do with football.

The Striker

"Let's pick one of the freshmen to make the speech!" shouted a Eureka senior. A dozen seniors sat around a long table, the time near midnight on the Eureka campus. The seniors were meeting to plot a campus revolt. They plotted to get rid of the school's president. Their battle cry was: "Wilson Must Go!" They would go on strike by refusing to attend classes. If Eureka's classrooms had no students in them, they told each other, president Bert Wilson would have to resign.

"Getting a freshman to make the speech—that's a good idea," said another senior. "The professors will listen to a freshman. Freshmen can't be accused of holding a grudge against the president. The freshmen just arrived on campus."

"What about Dutch Reagan? He's a freshman," someone said. "He did a lot of stage acting in high school. We need someone who can stand up on a stage and get everyone so excited they'll strike."

"Let's go ask Dutch to make the speech," another senior said.

Dutch had arrived on the Eureka campus, about a hundred miles from Dixon, only two months earlier. He looked at the sprawling green lawns and the brick, ivy-laced buildings, and a life-long love affair began.

"I fell head over heels in love with Eureka," he later wrote. "I wanted to get into that school so badly that it hurt when I thought about it."

Eureka was a small college—130 men, 120 women. Among its graduates were more than a dozen college presidents. Its football team played (and sometimes beat) some of the nation's best teams, including the University of Illinois' Fighting Illini.

Dutch talked to Eureka's athletic officials. He told them how he had smashed his high school's swimming records. They knew he had played for the Dixon High football team. With so few males at Eureka, football players were eagerly sought. The officials gave him an athletic scholarship that cut his tuition in half to $90.

Dutch also got a job washing dishes at a fraternity house. That paid for his meals at the fraternity house. But he had to pay $270 for his room at the house. College would cost him $360 for the year. He would have $40 of his $400 savings left for living expenses. Somehow, he told himself, he would make do.

Dutch decided to take a lot of economic and business subjects. He thought he might like to run his own business. He might own a store like the shoe emporium of his father's dreams.

He became a reporter for the campus newspaper. He and Mugs joined the school's dramatic club. Dutch dived into the Eureka swimming pool and raced ahead of juniors and seniors to win races for the swimming team. He set school records for the crawl and butterfly events that stood for years.

The church-owned college did not allow dances on the campus. Many Christian people of that time believed that dancing tempted young people into sinful acts. But Eureka students slipped off to the American Legion hall in town. They danced the fox trot and the Charleston, the two popular dances of a time that would be called The Jazz Age.

The school's president, Bert Wilson, began each school year with a speech that warned students against dancing. If caught dancing, he said, students would be thrown out of college. Angry students called it "The Dancing Speech." But in that fall of 1928, Wilson got them angrier. He told them that to save money the school would no longer offer certain courses. Many seniors needed those courses to graduate. Without those courses they could not get their diplomas. Four years of work and most of their parents' savings would be wasted.

"Wilson has to go!" seniors told each other. When they decided to strike by refusing to go to classes, they worried: suppose other students did attend classes? After all, even if those courses were no longer given, the freshmen, sophomores, and juniors could take other courses. They would graduate. The seniors had to get *all* the students to refuse to go to class. Then, seeing empty classrooms, Wilson would have to resign.

Dutch Reagan, the seniors decided, could make a speech that would arouse all the students and get them to join the strike. Just before midnight on a November night, the seniors rang the old college bell, the campus signal for a meeting in the chapel.

Seldom seen wearing glasses in public, Dutch poses with other members of the dramatic fraternity at Eureka. Mugs Cleaver is in the front row, far left. Moon stands second from right in the back row.
COURTESY EUREKA COLLEGE

Students and teachers rushed to the chapel, knowing the seniors were planning a strike.

People filled every seat and jammed the aisles. Others pressed against the windows to look inside. Dutch strode to the front of the chapel and began to speak.

He told the students why they should strike. Students, he said in a voice that rose and fell, had rights. His words rang across the crowded chapel. As he finished, students and teachers rose like one large body. They roared *"yes!"* to a strike. In the midst of the uproar one woman student fainted.

Students stopped going to classes. Teachers marked them present. President Wilson knew he was beat. A week after Dutch's speech, he resigned.

His speech that had made a crowd roar, Reagan said later, "was heady wine." He once wrote of the speech: "I discovered that night that an audience had a feel to it, and in the parlance of the theatre, the audience and I were together."

Dutch Reagan had also learned how exciting it was to ask people to follow you and hear them say, "Yes, we will follow you." And coaxing people to follow you is what politics is all about.

Becoming an All-American football hero remained his number one passion. He stood six feet tall and weighed 160 pounds, towering over most of the Golden Cyclones. But he was lighter than many and slower than most. The coach, Ralph McKenzie, made Dutch the team's fifth-string end. He never sent Dutch in for a single play that 1928 season.

"He was near-sighted, you know," the coach later told Anne Edwards in her book, *Early Reagan.* "Couldn't see. . . . End up at the bottom of the heap every time and missed the play because he couldn't see the man or the ball moving on him. Gotta say he was a regular at practice. And took his knocks. . . . He never quit . . . he was a plugger . . ."

Dutch, said the team's manager, "was the freshman who stuck with the football squad all fall although he never even got a first-class jersey."

In the dressing room after a game, Dutch often grabbed a broom stick and pretended he was speaking into a radio announcer's microphone. With his ringing voice, he told his audience: "And now the Golden Cyclones line up in the single-wing formation, the tailback . . ." The players listened, fascinated, as Dutch pretended to be a sportscaster who was announcing, play by play, the game they had just played.

"Never forgot a play either!" Coach McKenzie recalled. "He understood football. . . . He just couldn't execute on the playing field what he knew . . ."

Dutch got letters from home that worried him. Jack's Fashion Boot Store had few customers. Jack stumbled home drunk more often than he came home sober. Moon had refused to go to college—to Nelle's dismay. He had a job with a construction company, his pay less than ten dollars a week.

Dutch phoned Nelle. He said he'd come home and get a job. Absolutely not, she said. She wanted Moon and Dutch to graduate from college.

As 1929 began, the prices of shares on the stock market kept rising. On Wall Street people got rich overnight. But Europeans no longer bought American goods at a feverish pace. Bad times had come to Europe. People didn't have money to spend on big cars or radios. American factories began to lay off workers. Employers cut salaries of other workers. With less money in their pockets, Americans spent less.

In 1928 Al Smith had run against a Republican, Herbert Hoover. Jack, Dutch and Moon had plastered Al Smith for President signs all over Dixon. But Hoover won easily. He promised Americans that they would have "a chicken in every pot." But people in Dixon said, "The farmers are so poor, they can't feed the chickens."

Dutch and Mugs dated only each other at Eureka. In the evenings they strolled to a nearby graveyard, where Eureka's young people could sit by themselves. Dutch told Mugs that one day he would be a rich pro football player like Red Grange. Mugs could see that Dutch would never be a good football player. Anyway, she wanted to travel across Europe, learn foreign languages, and study in the museums and libraries of other countries. She didn't think of herself as the wife of a pro football player.

Dutch poses in the lineman's three-point stance. Like most young college men of the day, he parted his hair in the middle. The Depression forced many of his classmates to leave school to find work, including five of the class's six blacks.
COURTESY EUREKA COLLEGE

Mugs' parents came to Eureka. They treated Dutch and Mugs to a night at the theatre in nearby Rockford, Illinois. They saw the play *"Journey's End."* Laurence Olivier had been the star of the play when it had opened in England a year earlier. Dutch saw—for the first time in his life—professional actors and actresses performing on stage. He stared, entranced, at the leading man playing the role of Captain Stanhope.

"For two and a half hours," he said years later, "in some strange way I was also on stage. More than anything in life I wanted to speak his lines." He once confessed to reporter Lou Cannon: "I knew then that I wanted to be an actor, but it wasn't considered a way to make a living."

His freshman year ended in the spring of 1929. Dutch went back to Dixon. He put on his swimsuit with the words LIFE GUARD written across his chest. He cut more notches on the old log and saved $200 during the summer out of his $18-a-week pay.

That $200 would pay only half his college costs—and he'd be left with nothing to live on. He decided he had to give up college, football, acting, and—what hurt the most—Mugs. She was going back to Eureka. There, Dutch told himself, he would lose her to a college guy who was going to make a name for himself in the world.

A construction boss offered him a job. Dutch accepted. Now at least he could help Jack and Nelle. He knew his mother was disappointed. Moon still refused to go to college. And now Dutch had dropped out.

But what else could he do? He trudged over to Mugs' house one evening to say goodbye.

The Golden Cyclone

Dutch stared through the window of his tiny bedroom. Rain streamed down from dark skies. He was supposed to start work today with the construction crew. But he knew the work would be called off. The crew couldn't work in rain and mud.

Maybe somebody up there was telling him something. Maybe he shouldn't quit school. He glanced at his watch. Mugs would be leaving within the hour for Eureka.

Dutch left for Eureka with her. At school he told Coach McKenzie he didn't have enough money to pay for his tuition, room and board. The coach had come to admire this "plugger," as he called Dutch. The coach picked up the phone.

That evening Dutch called Nelle to tell her that the school would not charge him for his tuition. He could pay the school after he graduated—"my first experience with borrowing money," he later wrote. And he got free room and board for washing dishes in a women's dormitory. Washing dishes while chatting with pretty women, Dutch told pals, was a lot easier work than laboring with a construction crew.

Nelle clapped her hands with delight. Could Dutch, she asked, get the same kind of arrangement for Moon? Dutch said he would try. He told McKenzie how Moon caught long touchdown passes. Eureka needed a pass catcher. McKenzie agreed: Moon could come to Eureka and not pay until after he graduated.

33

FOOTBALL, 1930

The 1930 Golden Cyclones, their helmeted guard in the second row, third from the left. By now Dutch worked at a variety of jobs to earn money, including shoveling snow and raking leaves. He and Moon rarely went home for a visit because they couldn't afford the bus fare.
COURTESY EUREKA COLLEGE

But Moon told his mother he didn't want to go to college. Moon liked to drink beer after work and go out dancing in roadside taverns. He swaggered down Dixon streets. He thought that Dutch and college students didn't have any toughness.

Moon worked in a cement factory. His boss heard that Moon had said no to college. The boss told Moon, "If you're not smart enough to take the good thing your brother has fixed up for you, you're not smart enough to work for me." He fired Moon.

Moon arrived in Eureka the next day—to stay. Dutch talked to his fraternity brothers. They welcomed Moon to a room near Dutch's in the fraternity house.

Nelle cried with happiness. Years later she said, "I always knew Dutch would be a success, but Moon—that was another matter." She feared that Moon was too much like his father.

Coach McKenzie put both Reagans on his second team, Dutch

as a guard, Moon as an end. Eureka's best player was Bud Cole. He had bowled over ball carriers for Northwestern, one of the midwest's best teams, before coming to Eureka.

Bud admired Dutch's eagerness. He began to show Dutch how to "read" what an opponent was going to do.

"Knife in," he whispered to Dutch just before a play began, "they're going the other way!"

Dutch drove straight into the path of the ball carrier. He collided with the runner, knocking him to the turf. Dutch's vision was still blurry. But Cole was steering him to where all coaches want their tacklers to be—where the ball is.

That fall Eureka played a team in a town not far from Dixon. McKenzie booked rooms for the players at a hotel, but when the hotel clerk saw that two of the players were black, he said they could not sleep in the hotel. In those days, many restaurants and hotels in America would not serve black people.

An angry McKenzie stomped out of the hotel. Dutch asked what had happened. McKenzie told him and said, "We'll sleep the night in the bus."

Dutch said he thought the black players would be embarrassed. They might think, he told the coach, that it was their fault the team had to sleep on the bus.

"Dixon is not far away," Dutch said. "They can sleep at my house."

"Are you sure?" McKenzie asked.

Dutch was sure. He and the two black players rode by taxi to his house in Dixon. Nelle and Jack welcomed them warmly. The next morning Nelle cooked breakfast and Jack talked to them about the game. Nelle and Jack had raised their sons to believe you never disliked a person because of the color of his or her skin. But for the first time in his life, Dutch had seen the mindless cruelty of racial prejudice.

In that fall of 1929, a few Wall Street investors began to sell shares of stock in United States companies. The investors thought bad times were coming, and that the companies could lose money, making their stock worth a lot less money.

Others began to sell. As more shares were put up for sale, the price of shares fell. Fear began to spread: *I'll get less money for my shares than I paid for them.* Fear turned within days to panic. Millions of people threw their shares onto the market.

Stock prices nose-dived. And on one "Black Thursday" in October of 1929, the stock market crashed—a crash heard around the world.

Millions of Americans—clerks, housewives, widows, plumbers, shop owners—awoke the next morning to learn that most or all of their life's savings had vanished. They could not afford to buy high-priced things like cars or even a new radio. The factories that made high-priced items shut down and fired workers. Those workers could not buy even medium-priced items, so those factories shut down, throwing more workers onto the streets. By 1930 and 1931 millions of men and women were hoarding their last dimes and quarters to feed themselves and their children. By 1932 one out of every four American workers did not have a job.

Millions had no money to buy overcoats and shoes. Jack's Fashion Boot Store closed. He was lucky enough to get a job in a run-down shoe store in Springfield, Illinois, about two hundred miles from Dixon. He lived in a cheap hotel infested with fleas and rats. Nelle sewed clothes in a women's store for $14 a week. Often she had to walk miles to deliver a package.

She lived in one room. Her "kitchen" was an electric hot plate. Her local grocery store refused to let her buy any more food on credit—she owed too much. Desperate, she wrote to Dutch. He dug $50 out of his savings as a lifeguard and sent it to her.

The Golden Cyclones played a team in Springfield, where Jack worked. Dutch and Moon now played on the first team. They invited Jack to dine with the team. Jack told comical stories about traveling as a shoe salesman. The players roared with laughter.

He turned serious as the talk turned to what Americans now called "hard times"—The Great Depression. "This country isn't going to get better," he told the players, "until the Republicans are shooed out of office." Grinning impishly, he lifted one foot in a kicking gesture. "Yes," he said loudly. "We'll S-H-O-E 'em out."

McKenzie laughed. "Your father," he told Dutch, "sure is a red-hot Democrat."

"So am I," Dutch said.

On dates he and Mugs went to see the new talking motion pictures. Stars of the new "talkies" included Jean Harlow and Marlene Dietrich, Douglas Fairbanks, Jr., and Dutch's favorite, a tall, broad-shouldered former All-American football player, Johnny Mack Brown. He played gun-slinging cowboys such as Billy the Kid.

After the movies, Dutch and Mugs strolled to the nearby graveyard with other couples. They talked late into the night. Dutch often swung the talk to politics, although the subject held little interest to Mugs. Dutch liked to repeat what the new governor of New York, Franklin Delano Roosevelt, was saying. Dutch told Mugs that Roosevelt was right when he said that

The members of Eureka's sophomore class gather for a group picture, Reagan on the far left in the back row. During Dutch's junior year, Mugs attended the University of Illinois. Dutch got a case of what he called "leading-ladyitus" with the pretty co-star of a play, but he got over it when Mugs came back to Eureka for her senior year.
COURTESY EUREKA COLLEGE

President Hoover wasn't doing enough to help the unemployed get food and jobs.

In classrooms Dutch slipped by with Cs and an occasional B. He rarely studied in the evenings. He kept busy being a football player in the fall, running for offices like the student senate and president of his class, cheerleading for the basketball team, acting in school plays, or being an editor of the yearbook.

"He would take a book the night before the test," Moon once said, "and in about a quick hour he would thumb through it and photograph those pages and write a good test."

Dutch became what was called a BMOC—Big Man On Campus. Classmates elected him president of the senior class. He smashed most of Eureka's swimming records, and coached the team his junior and senior years. He was president of the school's Booster Club. He led the basketball cheerleaders. He presided over the student senate. And he ran onto gridirons to start at right guard for the Golden Cyclones. He proudly wore the gold and red uniform on the field, his big "E" on a sweater on campus.

"Everyone admired Dutch," a classmate once said. "I can't think of anyone who disliked him."

"He was a leader," McKenzie said, "and he used his power well."

He caught the eyes of both men and women. He had a way of striding across the stage in plays that made people look at him even when another actor was speaking. At parties he stood out—tall, slim, blue eyes flashing behind his tanned lifeguard's face. His wavy hair, parted in the middle, was burnished chestnut brown by the sun. He looked people straight in the eye as he spoke, an Irish lilt to his laughter. Even older people felt flattered that he had given them his attention.

Mugs looked at Dutch with mixed feelings. She admired his handsome face and strong, lean body. But she worried that he didn't study hard. It seemed to her that he had little ambition. And he didn't share her curiosity about the world outside Eureka or her desire to travel. "He was a leader," she said years later. "Still, I didn't think he'd end up accomplishing anything."

"Drama, sports and politics were my greatest interests at

Eureka's best swimmer poises on a springboard. "I don't believe he ever swam in a pool before," said football coach Ralph McKinzie. But once he got used to a pool, said the coach, "nothing could hold him back. . . . But he had this dream I guess of becoming a big football star."
COURTESY EUREKA COLLEGE

Ron (left) plays a Greek shepherd boy in *Aria da Capo*, an anti-war play in which he was cruelly strangled by an enemy—the kind of death scene most actors love. The Greek maiden posing in front of him is played by Mugs.
COURTESY EUREKA COLLEGE

Eureka," Reagan once said. When he talked politics, Dutch often said he was a pacifist. He thought America had been tricked by Britain into entering World War I.

He won a role in a play, *Aria da Capo*, by Edna St. Vincent Millay. The play showed the foolishness of war. His part was as a Greek shepherd who is strangled to death. The "strangler" was his football tutor, Bud Cole.

Every actor likes to die slowly on stage. All eyes fix on him during his death agonies. "No actor," Dutch once said, "can ask for more" than a good death scene.

The Eureka players went to Northwestern University to compete against acting groups from colleges across the nation. Eureka's *Aria da Capo* won second place. Then, as hundreds of young actors and actresses waited expectantly, an announcer called out the names of the winners of the awards for individual performances.

"Ronald Reagan!" said the announcer. Dutch leaped out of his seat and rushed onto the stage to accept the award.

A senior in the spring of 1932, Dutch knew he would never become an All-American. But he now stood head and shoulders above the other students at Eureka. "If you make it" at a small school, he once said, "it's because your fellow students know you, not because they don't (know you). And if you can make it under those circumstances, you can make it anywhere."

Years later he returned to Eureka (whose sports center is now named for Ronald and Neil Reagan). "Everything good that has happened to me—everything," he said, "started here on this campus."

He had not become an All-American, true. But he had learned a lot about football. He had begun to learn it literally from the ground up back in Dixon as a scrub player trampled black and blue. He had learned its nuances sitting next to McKenzie on the bench, and then as Bud Cole sent him left, right and straight ahead. All of the bruises, all of the work, all of the patience would soon be rewarded. The payoff would give Dutch Reagan his first lift upward to a place no all-American has ever reached.

The Sportscaster

A cool September breeze rippled the water near the river's shore. Dutch sat on the lifeguard stand, his eyes sweeping over the dozen shivering bathers. The summer of 1932 was coming to an end—and so was Dutch's career as a lifeguard.

Dutch had graduated in June. At graduation he and Mugs held a strand of woven ivy between them to show they would stay connected. "Connected" couples usually married.

Dutch needed a year-round job. But this was a time when more people wanted jobs than at anytime in America's history. Jack didn't have a job. Moon was going back to Eureka for his senior year. The family lived on Nelle's $14 a week and $10 a week from Dutch. He put the other $8 of his lifeguard's pay into savings.

The family squeezed into a two-room apartment. Dutch slept on the couch. They had no kitchen. A neighbor cooked their food and passed the meals through an open window.

The Reagans were among the lucky ones in Dixon. Families went to bed each night hungry and cold, their last nickels and dimes gone for food and fuel.

Jack plastered "Elect Roosevelt" signs all over Dixon. New York's Franklin Delano Roosevelt had won the Democratic nomination for President. FDR, as newspaper headlines called him, promised "A new deal for the American people."

A new deal! A new beginning! Jack told people in Dixon that "a new deal" would mean a President who cared about farmers, shop owners, and laborers. "Vote Roosevelt," he told listeners, "or vote for Hoover and ruin." Dutch wore a "Vote FDR" button on his lifeguard's swimsuit.

In that fall of 1932, Dutch also looked at the prices of shares on the stock market. That summer the prices had sunk to their lowest level in the century. But by fall they had begun to climb—and twenty years later they would rise to their 1929 levels.

Years later, while writing a magazine article on the stock market, I wrote to President Reagan and asked him if he had thought about investing money in the stock market during that summer of 1932 when there were so many bargains.

He wrote back:

"Yes, I was aware of the stock market. My degree was in economics and part of our class assignment was keeping track of a list of stocks on a daily basis. As I recall, the July [1932] drop [to a new all-century low] didn't seem all that important after going through the Black Thursday in '29 and the depression years since. I did, however, have one stock I checked that by July was down to less than a half dollar."

He was tempted to buy that stock, President Reagan wrote to me. When the Depression was over, he told himself, the stock would be worth many times what he paid for it in 1932.

"But I resisted the temptation," the President added. "I could save about $200 over the entire summer . . . I felt I would need all of that for the job hunt and I was right. But I also recall that had I risked a little of that $200 I might have made about 30- or 40-to-1 profit in the next few years."

Late in that summer of 1932, he heard about what he considered a dream job, selling sporting goods at Dixon's Montgomery Ward store. The job paid $12.50 a week, top pay at Dixon stores. A horde of young men applied. The store narrowed its choice to two men—Dutch and another local athlete. In what he later called the most disappointing day of his life, Dutch was told that the other man had won the job.

Some forty-five years later he went back to Dixon. A man stopped him and said, "You don't remember me, do you?"

"Sure I do," Ronald Reagan said. "You're the guy who beat me out of that job at Montgomery Ward."

At his lifeguard stand one day, Dutch talked to B.J. Fraser, who had asked him to act in high school plays. Dutch told Fraser that he sometimes thought about becoming an actor. But he knew people in Dixon would say he was crazy.

"Get a job communicating," Fraser told him. "You're good at it."

Radio sets had come into most American homes. Americans listened to comedians such as Eddie Cantor. They heard stage performers most people had never seen—Al Jolson, Fanny Brice, W.C. Fields. Teenagers listened at night to the records of crooners like Bing Crosby. Kids and adults listened to baseball games from far away Chicago and college football games from Iowa and even Minnesota.

Dutch decided he would try to be a radio announcer of baseball and football games—the sportscaster he had so often pretended to be. He told Mugs he would go to Chicago and try to get a job as an announcer at one of the big radio stations.

Mugs shook her head at what seemed another impossible dream. A year later she went to Europe with her sister and there met a handsome American diplomat. She sent back an engagement ring Dutch had given her and married the diplomat. She would go on to live the life of travel and study she had yearned for.

In that letter to this author in 1985, President Reagan also wrote:

". . . At that time [in 1932] the government was putting announcements on the radio telling people not to leave home looking for work because there was none. Well, I wasn't going to listen to them."

Pessimists saw 1932 and the Great Depression as the beginning of the end for the United States as a democracy. They predicted that poor people would set up, as they had a few years earlier in Russia, a Communist state. Dutch, the optimist, was looking to "when the depression was over." And he wasn't going to listen to what any government told him: he was going to Chicago to look for a job.

Years later, newly-elected President Reagan looked back on his life and said that the most important year of his life had been 1932, the year he had reached up with his own hands and begun to lift himself from poverty.

President Reagan added that the Great Depression had been the single most important event of his life. Someone once said, "When you are born poor, you are always poor," always worried about money. Ronald Reagan would always spend his money carefully. Like most people who came out of the Great Depression, he could never throw away money. He always worried that he might be poor again.

Dutch hitchhiked to Chicago. He tramped from one radio station to the next, asking for a job. He was told: "Go back to a small town and get experience."

He hitchhiked back to Dixon. He circled on a map the nearby small towns that had radio stations. He borrowed his father's old car and drove to Davenport, Iowa, some seventy-five miles away. He asked for a job at station WOC. The manager, Peter MacArthur, told Dutch that only yesterday he had interviewed ninety-four applicants for an announcer's job and hired one of them. The station had no other jobs open.

Dutch turned away and growled, "How does anyone get a chance as a sports announcer if you can't even get a job in a radio station?"

Sports? MacArthur called to Dutch to come back to his desk. A Scotchman with a burr to his voice, MacArthur asked, "Do ye perhaps know football?"

"I played football for eight years," Dutch said.

"Do ye think ye could tell me about a game and make me see it?"

Since high school, pretending a broom stick was a microphone, Dutch had played make-believe sports announcer. Now he had to try to sound like a real sports announcer—in front of a real mike—with maybe a job at stake.

Beads of sweat glistened on his forehead as he sat before a microphone in a small studio. MacArthur listened in a nearby booth. Dutch decided to describe a Eureka game he had played in a year earlier.

"We are going into the fourth quarter now," Dutch began. "A chill wind is blowing in through the end of the stadium . . ."

His memory recalling every play of that quarter, Dutch described how Eureka won. His voice vibrant with excitement, he shouted into the mike: "Dutch Reagan blocks a tackler and there goes the ball carrier down the sideline. . . ." Actually, he had missed the tackler.

Dutch finished twenty minutes of non-stop talking, his shirt soaked with sweat. MacArthur burst into the studio and shouted, "Ye did great."

But MacArthur had no jobs open. He offered Dutch $5 and bus fare to Iowa City to broadcast—with another announcer—a University of Iowa game the next Saturday. Jack and Nelle listened at home. Eyes shining, they heard the announcer say: "and now to bring you the play-by-play action, here is Ronald Reagan."

"How do you do, ladies and gentlemen," Dutch began. "We are speaking to you from high atop the Memorial Stadium at the University of Iowa, looking down from the west stands. It's a gusty day with the wind out of the north."

The other announcer took over for the second quarter. Dutch came back for the third quarter. Dutch knew much more than the other announcer about what it was like to block, tackle, hit and be hit. MacArthur sat nearby, listening. The fourth quarter began. MacArthur told the other announcer: "Let the kid finish the game."

Dutch's pay went up to $10 a game. He broadcast three more Iowa games that fall. A *Chicago Tribune* critic wrote after one rainy game that Dutch's "crisp account of the muddy struggle . . . and his quick tongue seemed to be as fast as the plays."

That fall twenty-one year old Ronald Wilson Reagan voted for the first time. He voted for FDR, who beat Hoover easily. Millions of poor people waited anxiously for Roosevelt to take office in March, 1933, and give them "the new deal"—that new chance—he had promised.

As 1933 began, Dutch had only a few dollars left of his $200 lifeguard savings. He asked for a job swinging an ax as a highway laborer, but didn't get it. Then MacArthur called. Dutch's face lit up as he heard MacArthur say he was hired as a $100 a month staff announcer on WOC.

Dutch moved to Davenport. He sent $5 a week to Nelle and a few dollars a week to Moon at Eureka. He began to repay the money he owed the college. Christian church members believe in "tithing," paying ten percent of your income to the church. Dutch sent $10 a month to the Christian church in Dixon. He would tithe ten percent of his income to the church the rest of his life.

Dutch played records and read commercials. Advertisers complained to MacArthur: "That kid reads my commercials so stiffly no one believes what he's saying."

Dutch had trouble reading the commercials from a written script. He stumbled over words. He took the scripts home and memorized the words. The next day, like an actor in a play, he

Dutch Reagan delivers a laugh line at the WHO mike in Des Moines. When he did his re-creations of Cub games, he had never seen a big league baseball game. But he did make an overnight trip to Chicago where he memorized what Wrigley Field looked like.
COURTESY REAGAN PRESIDENTIAL MATERIALS STAFF

read the words as though he had just thought them up. He sounded as though he believed every word he said about an advertiser's product. The advertisers began to smile.

Dutch told people that a gift from God—his ringing voice— was not enough. You had to work hard to get all you could out of that gift.

WOC also owned WHO, a more powerful station, in Des Moines. The station transferred Dutch to WHO. He began to broadcast "re-creations" of the Chicago Cubs baseball games to listeners all over the midwest. Most radio stations could not afford to send sportscasters to games. So they broadcast these "re-creations."

Dutch sat before a mike in a small booth at WHO in Des Moines. At Wrigley Field in Chicago, a telegraph man tapped out in code a pitch-by-pitch report of the game. At WHO another telegraph man decoded the report and typed, on a slip of paper, what had happened on each pitch. He handed the slip to Dutch. If Dutch read "S2-S" that meant the pitch had been strike two, the batter having swung at the pitch.

A record played the sounds of cheers and other crowd noises as Dutch excitedly described hits, runs and errors. "The Giants' Hubbell pitches, Galan swings . . . there's a drive to right field . . ."

"You just couldn't believe that you weren't actually there at the ballpark," a WHO executive once said, "Of course, he knew baseball and that helped."

The Cubs were playing the St. Louis Cardinals one day. "Billy Jurges is at bat," Dutch was saying. He reached for the slip of paper. He read: "The telegraph's gone dead."

Dutch didn't know what had happened to the pitch—he had told his listeners that the pitch was on its way to the batter. Thinking quickly, Dutch said, "Jurges fouls it off. Strike one."

He stared helplessly at the telegraph man, who shrugged. The line to Chicago was still dead.

For the next few minutes Dutch described how Jurges fouled off pitch after pitch. One foul ball almost landed fair for a home run. Another foul landed in the grandstand seats and Dutch described—as long as he dared—how two kids fought for the ball. But how long could Jurges keep "fouling" pitches? He'd set a record for fouls—fouls that Dutch was making up.

Suddenly the telegraph man started typing. Dutch grabbed the slip. He had to stop himself from laughing. It read that Jurges had popped out on the first ball pitched. "Jurges pops out," Dutch told his audience, and he hoped they would forget about all those foul balls that had never been fouled.

By now, 1936, millions were still unemployed. But the New Deal, as FDRs administration was now called, had given people hope. FDR and his New Dealers believed that the U.S. government should give money and food to the poor. It was called home relief, now known as welfare. Most important, said New Dealers, the government should hire workers. With their wages they could buy their own food. Then they wouldn't need home relief.

FDR put millions to work for the government. They built bridges, roads, parks and tunnels. They saved money and bought stoves, cars, refrigerators and radios. To make those products, companies hired more workers. Those workers had money to buy products. More factories opened and hired more workers. The worst of the Great Depression was over.

The government gave Jack a job. He hired people to work on New Deal projects. But three heart attacks had left him too weak to work. For the rest of their lives, Jack and Nelle would live on money sent to them by Dutch.

Dutch now earned $75 a week—at a time when $20 a week was princely pay. Dutch sent $25 a week to Nelle. He rented a small apartment in Des Moines. He dated women who worked at WHO as well as co-eds from Drake University.

One girl friend liked to ride horses. Dutch took riding lessons. Soon he was riding on galloping horses across the countryside. That began a life-long love affair with horses and riding. "Ever since boyhood," he once said, "there was always a little bit of Tom Mix in me."

He saved money to buy a sleek new convertible. The car's top down, he streaked at night to roadside taverns where young people laughed, drank and danced until dawn. Dutch had seen close up what alcohol can do. He sipped one or two drinks during a night, rarely more. With a pretty blond or brunette at his side, he soon became known as that "dashing young blade around town."

Moon had graduated from Eureka but couldn't find a job. He lived with Dutch in Des Moines for a year and a half, supported by Dutch. Then Dutch got Moon a job at the radio station as a sportscaster. That started a career for Moon as a salesman for radio stations. An affable good-time fellow like Jack, Moon sold time on radio to advertisers. By the 1980s Neil Reagan had become a millionaire radio-TV-advertising executive on the west coast.

FDR won again in 1936. He got more votes than any President ever. Again Dutch wore a "Vote for FDR button"—this time on a new, expensive sports jacket.

With friends, Dutch liked to imitate FDR, his political idol, making one of his "fireside" speeches by radio. Copying FDR's Harvard-bred accent, he recited FDR's most famous words, delivered in the darkest days of the Depression: "All we have to feahhh is feahhh itself."

Dutch and Jack had always believed that people should help themselves. Going on the dole, they had believed, was shameful. But the Great Depression had been a disaster—like the crash of an airliner that injures hundreds. Instead of an airliner, the national economy had crashed, injuring millions.

Just as airliner victims need quick help, so did the victims of the Depression—and only the government could get them quickly on their feet. FDR's New Deal government, Jack and Dutch now said, had been right to help the Depression's injured—the poor, the homeless, the unemployed—by handing out food, money and jobs. FDR's New Deal government had put Americans back on their feet. Dutch, and millions of other Americans, would be forever grateful.

Dutch interviewed celebrities on WHO when they came to Des Moines. A Hollywood starlet, Joy Hodges, came to town to get publicity for a new movie. Dutch interviewed her, first making clear to her that his name was pronounced Ray-gun, not Ree-gun.

Joy saw handsome men in Hollywood every day. She thought Dutch as handsome as any Hollywood actor she had ever seen.

"Well, Miss Hodges," Dutch began the interview, "how does it feel to be a movie star?"

"Well, Mr. Ray-gun," Joy said, "you may know one day."

Joy would always remember how soon she turned out to be right.

The Movie Hero

The silvery streamliner streaked across the California desert toward Los Angeles. On this early spring day in 1937, the train carried twenty-six-year-old Dutch toward his first face-to-face meetings with the ball players whose games he had been describing all last summer—the Chicago Cubs.

The Cubs trained on an island off Los Angeles. Dutch had convinced his WHO bosses that he should study the team during spring training in 1937 for that summer's re-created games.

He still thought a lot about acting. "I'd rather act than anything else," he once told friends at WHO.

Arriving in Los Angeles, he called Joy Hodges, who was singing with a band. He invited her to lunch, and asked her if she thought he could be a movie actor.

Joy asked him to stand up and take off his glasses. She stared at Dutch's six foot, tree-trunk-hard frame, the chestnut hair, the clean-cut face. "It was clear," she later wrote, "that he was *very handsome.* I told him never to put those glasses on again."

Joy sent him to her agent, who got jobs for actors. Dutch's poise and appearance impressed the agent, who called the Warner Brothers Studio, one of Hollywood's biggest. The studio agreed to give Dutch a screen test.

A Warner Brothers director placed Dutch in front of a camera and asked him to read lines to an actress. A nervous Dutch read the lines stiffly. He thought he was terrible. The director told Dutch the studio would need weeks to judge the screen test.

Dutch rode back to Des Moines on the train. He walked into the WHO office and was given a telegram that had just arrived from the Hollywood agent.

Warner Offers Contract Seven Years . . . Starting At $200 A Week. What Shall I Do?

Dutch shot back a telegram:

Sign Before They Change Their Minds.

Late in May of 1937 Dutch packed all of his belongings into his new convertible. He waved goodbye to his parents and Moon, promising to call when he got to Hollywood. Six days later, grimy with desert dust, he drove down Hollywood Boulevard. It was called "The Street of Broken Dreams," the street where thousands like Dutch had come yearning to be rich and famous and ended up broke and bitter.

Studios often changed the names of young actors. They gave the actors alluring names. Archibald Leach, for example, became Cary Grant. But Ronald Reagan, studio officials thought, had a nice ring to it. Instead of losing his name, Dutch Reagan got back the name he had been given at birth twenty-six years earlier.

Other actors called him Ron or Ronnie, often startling someone used to being called Dutch. (But even after the name Ronald Reagan had become known around the globe, people in Dixon still called him Dutch.)

Ronald Reagan immediately began work, playing the leading role in *Love Is On the Air*. Fittingly enough, he played a radio broadcaster. The broadcaster tricks a gang of crooks into confessing inside a radio studio. The crooks don't know their words are being broadcast and cops then arrest the crooks.

In those days movie goers wanted two movies for their twenty-five cent tickets. The two movies were called a double feature. The second movie was called a B movie. It featured low-salaried "contract players" like Ronald Reagan and had been made

The newly re-christened Ronald Reagan whispers into the ear of his co-star, June Travis, in a publicity photo for his first movie, *Love Is On the Air*. He caught another case of "leading-ladyitus" with the green-eyed June, dating her during the making of the movie. But the romance ended when the movie shooting ended—three weeks later.
COURTESY HERMAN DARVICK

quickly and cheaply. The double feature's A movie presented high-salaried stars like Bette Davis, Jimmy Cagney, Pat O'Brien and Humphrey Bogart. They were paid as much as $3,000 a week at a time when bank presidents got no more than $500 a week.

Contract players ate at the studio's lunch room side by side with the stars. Ron stared, open-mouthed, at the stars. He was so awed he couldn't talk to Jimmy Cagney, even to remind Cagney that he had once interviewed him for WHO in Des Moines.

Cagney and his best friend, Pat O'Brien, liked to talk about sports. They knew Ron had been a sportscaster. They invited Ron to lunch with them. Soon Ron and other male stars—Bogart, Edward G. Robinson, George Brent among them—lunched together and argued whether Southern California would beat UCLA the following Saturday.

Ron puzzled other contract players. Waiting for a scene to be shot, they liked to talk about what roles they might get in their next B picture. Ron liked to talk about politics and current events. One day he said to actor Larry Williams:

"What would you say is the current population of Formosa?"

"Ronnie, I don't know things like that."

"Right. Most Americans don't. No need to apologize."

"I'm glad."

"I've got the population figures right here, but before I give it to you . . ." Ron then went off on a long speech about the history of Formosa and China and how the United States might become embroiled in a war with a Far East power like Japan.

Ron talked politics even when he dated pretty actresses like Joy Hodges, who had fallen in love with him. But to Ron, Joy was just a friend—"to my regret," she later said.

They rode horses together. "We discussed politics more than any other subject," she once recalled. "He was a passionate Democrat and I a Republican, and we used to go round and round about that . . . He loved anything and everything about government, history and politics."

When Ron did talk movies with other actors, he talked about the business side of Hollywood. He argued loudly that studio bosses were unfair to actors. Like all film actors, he belonged to the Screen Actors Guild (SAG). It was a labor union. All contract players like Ron had to sign seven-year contracts with a studio. The seven-year contract enslaved actors, SAG had argued—and Ron agreed. The actors could work only for that one studio for seven years. The studio set their pay. And the studio could, at almost any time, fire the actor.

Ron was angrily criticizing the seven-year contract one day. His agent overheard. "There's nothing you can do about it, Ronnie," the agent said.

A grin spread across Ron's face. But it wasn't the boyish grin that was making hearts beat faster for millions of movie-going girls and women. It was a wolfish, hungry grin. "Well," he said slowly, "a way has to be figured to turn that around."

In 1937 and 1938 Ron made almost a dozen B movies. He always played the leading man who tripped up the villains and won the heart of the leading lady. He once said of his early career: "Remember the guy in movies who rushes into the phone booth, pushes his hat to the back of his head while the tails of his trench coat are still flying, drops a nickel into the box, dials a few numbers, then says, 'Gimme the city desk. I've got a story that'll split this town wide open.' That was me."

Movie directors admired him. He came to the set on time. He always memorized his lines and the lines of the other actors in the scene with him. As B.J. Fraser had taught him, he asked himself, "Why? Why are these characters doing these things that the script says they are doing?"

He did have to learn how to kiss for the movies. "Your lips should barely touch," a director told him. "If you really kiss a girl, it shoves her face out of shape."

Movie critics praised his acting. Said one: Reagan has "charm and vitality." Another wrote that he "impresses and handles his fists well." Hundreds of letters to Ron poured into the studio each week from fans asking for his autograph or a signed photo.

A year after he came to Hollywood, Ron called Jack and Nelle and told them to leave Dixon and come to Hollywood. He bought them a home, the first they had ever owned. Jack had been weakened by another heart attack. Ron got him a job behind a desk at the studio opening mail and sending out photos, including ones of his son.

All that fan mail impressed Ron's bosses at Warner. They put him in an A movie, his first, titled *Brother Rat*. It was a story about cadets at a military college. Ron played one of the cadets. In the movie he dated the daughter of the college's commander, a pert and pixyish blond played by another contract player named Jane Wyman.

The director told Ron and Jane to go to a photo studio for what are called "stills," posed photographs. The photographer came late. An angry Jane snapped that as usual the contract players were being pushed around.

"It's just a mistake," Ron said in a calming voice. "It's no one's fault."

That impressed Jane. "It didn't seem possible," she later said, "that a man could have so even a disposition . . ."

"I was drawn to him at once," she said. "He was such a sunny person." But when she talked to him, he seemed not to be interested in her. At the time she was divorcing her first husband. To the religious Ron, she was somebody else's wife.

His roving eyes had caught sight of a saucy brunette who was also playing a part in *Brother Rat*. Her name was Susan Hayward. As Jane bit her lip, Ronald joshed with Susan most every day between scenes of the movie.

But after Jane's divorce, he asked her for a date. Within six months they were dating only each other. He told other actors she was "a good scout, nice to be with." But they guessed he had fallen in love.

Jane Wyman's real name was Sarah Jane Fulks. Born in St. Joseph, Missouri, she was six years younger than Ron. "I grew up with hurt and bewilderment," she once said. She was strictly raised by her mother, her father having died when Sarah Jane was eleven. Her mother moved to Los Angeles. Sarah Jane took dancing lessons and, at seventeen, won a job dancing in a chorus line of a movie musical. She earned less than a thousand dollars a year but somehow supported herself and her mother. In 1936, Warner delighted her by signing her as a contract player at $65 a week. She stepped out of the chorus line to play dizzy blonds. When she met Ronnie, as she always called him, "for the first time, I really trusted someone."

Jane was suddenly stricken by a stomach ailment and taken to a hospital. Ron went to see her. Jane's mother, fearful of losing a daughter, stopped him from entering her room. Ron came back the next day and forced his way into the room. When he left, he and Jane were engaged to be married.

They married early in 1940. They moved into Jane's apartment near Hollywood Boulevard and lived the movie actor's life: up at dawn for 6:00 A.M. dates at makeup, home at dusk for 8:00 P.M. dinners and early to bed. On weekends Jane liked to play golf. They joined a country club, found that the country club refused to admit Jews, and resigned. They joined another club and soon made friends at the club with comedians George Burns and Jack Benny, both of whom were Jewish.

Ronald Reagan had made a dozen movies, all B pictures

except for *Brother Rat*, and in that A movie his part was minor. The dashing Errol Flynn reigned as the king of pictures at Warner's. He played swashbuckling pirates and hard-riding cowboys. "I am the Errol Flynn of B pictures," Ron said disgustedly.

Then he heard that Warner's would make a movie of the life of Knute Rockne. Rockne had been the coach of the Notre Dame football team in the 1920s. The team had won championships, many of its players All-Americans. One of its most famous players was George (The Gipp) Gipper. A few months after his last game, Gipp lay dying of pneumonia. He turned to Rockne and whispered, "Coach, if there is ever a game you want the team to win, tell them to win this one for the Gipper." Then he died.

Ron Reagan wanted that part as badly as he had ever wanted anything in his life. He had played football, he knew football. And he knew a great death scene when he saw one.

His pal, Pat O'Brien, would play Rockne. Ron begged O'Brien: Could he play the Gipper?

"They may want a name actor," O'Brien said doubtfully.

"I can play the part, I won't let you down if I get the assignment."

O'Brien looked at Ron's eager, college-boy face. "Let me talk to Jack Warner," he said.

The Gipper

Pat O'Brien knew Ron was nervous. They stood facing a movie camera on a football field near the Warner's studio. The genial always-smiling Pat had jollied the studio bosses into giving Ron a screen test to see if he looked on the screen like an All-American football player.

Ron had studied Knute Rockne's diaries. He had tried to learn all he could about the character of George Gipp.

He wore football pants, shoulder pads, a helmet and a jersey. He and O'Brien would read the lines from an important scene in the *Knute Rockne—All-American* script. In this scene Rockne discovers how great this freshman Gipp would be.

"Action!" shouted a director. The camera whirred. Pat handed Ron a football and told him to try to carry the ball into a wall of hulking Notre Dame linemen.

Ron took the ball and said cockily, "How far?"

When Gipp said that—and then ran through the Notre Dame line—Rockne knew that George Gipp could carry the ball against anyone as far as his legs could carry him.

Studio officials applauded when they viewed the screen test. Ron looked and acted, they said, like a football star.

Ron appeared on the screen for only a few minutes as George Gipp in *Knute Rockne—All-American*. But movie goers laughed when he asked Rockne: "How far?" And they wept when the dying Gipp said to Rockne, "Win one for the Gipper." In the movie's climactic scene, O'Brien, as Rockne, begs his team to "win this one for the Gipper"—and the Fighting Irish charge out onto the field to win.

Playing The Gipper, Ron said, was an actor's dream: "A great entrance, an action middle, and a death scene to finish it up."

The role was Ron's first important one in an A picture. Fans sent Ron more letters asking him for autographs than to any other Warner's actor except Errol Flynn. The *Los Angeles Times* wrote: "It will behoove Warner's to set about getting good roles for Mr. Reagan."

His salary soared. By 1940 Warner's paid him $1,000 a week and it paid Jane $500 a week. Together they earned more in a week than many Americans earned in a year. But Ron could not forget the scariness of poverty.

He insisted that they pay off big bills that Jane had run up when she was single. That left her with $500 in the bank. "That's the beginning of our savings account," he told her.

He set up a budget so they would not spend too much and so their bank account would grow. "He has a fit if we don't pay all our bills right away," Jane told a friend. They began to put into the bank about half of their $1,500 a week salaries.

Jane had made a musical movie with Dick Powell. A singing star, Powell—Richard to his friends—had switched roles and now played tough-guy detectives. Intelligent and ambitious, he hoped to become a studio boss—and years later he would co-own a studio. He was married to June Allyson, who usually played the role of a sweet, demure girl. June was just as demure and sweet off-screen. A $3,000 a week star, she had a doll-like face and twinkling eyes that were often seen on the covers of movie-fan magazine.

Stars like June Allyson and Dick Powell seldom became pals with contract players like Ron and Jane. But June liked Jane. Jane Wyman played brash, wisecracking blonds in movies. But off-screen she was much like the gracious, friendly June. Soon the Powells and the Reagans were close friends.

"Arguing politics drew them together," June once said of Ron and her husband. "It was a riot to listen to Ronnie, a staunch

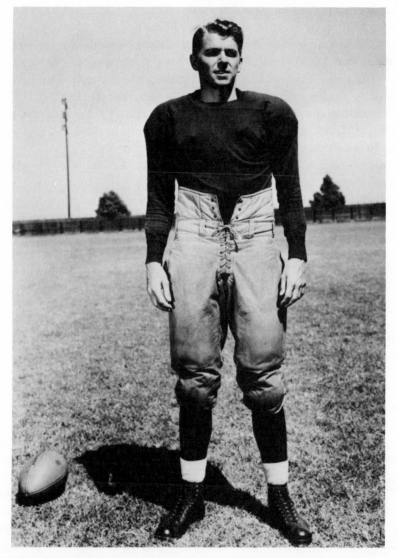

Dutch looks like the All-American he always wished he had been for this publicity photo as George Gipp for *Knute Rockne—All-American.* When *Knute Rockne—All-American* was previewed at the University of Notre Dame, Ron took his father, a devoted Notre Dame fan, to the festive affair. Jack delighted priests, nuns and Pat O'Brien with stories of his shoe-salesman days.
COURTESY REAGAN PRESIDENTIAL MATERIALS STAFF

Democrat, trying to convert Richard, while Richard argued just as hard to turn Ronnie into a Republican."

In 1940, one question was hotly debated in millions of American homes: Should the United States go to war? A year earlier the guns of World War II had roared across Europe. The bullet-spitting tanks and planes of Germany's dictator, Adolf Hitler, had conquered Poland and France. England now stood alone against Hitler, a besieged island. Its people huddled in shelters as Hitler's planes bombed and burned their cities.

Many Americans wanted to rush help to England, a sister democracy. They wanted to send guns, planes and ships. Some of these people, called interventionists, even wanted to send soldiers to invade Europe and destroy Hitler. If Hitler were not beaten, interventionists argued, he would destroy England and then the United States, the world's last powerful democracy. Americans would be Hitler's slaves and die in his death camps.

Millions of others called themselves isolationists. They said America should mind its own business. "We fought World War I to make the world safe for democracy," they argued, "and what did it get us? Just another European war. Let's stay out of their bloody messes."

President Roosevelt sided with Americans who wanted to help England. He urged the Congress to send ships and guns—but not soldiers—to help England. And in 1940 he decided to run for a third term. Republicans roared that FDR wanted to turn himself into a dictator like Hitler or Russia's Josef Stalin. But Democrats argued that the country needed a strong leader like FDR to guide the country around World War II.

No Democrat argued louder than Ron for a third term for Roosevelt. "Reagan idolized him as some people would idolize a film star," another actor said. Dick Powell told Ron that while FDR might be a great man, the people around him in the White House were radical and Communists. They wanted, argued Powell, to turn America into a Communist slave state like Communist Russia.

Ron stuck to his guns and defended FDR with a blizzard of facts. He pored over newspapers and political journals to back up his arguments in debates. Powell told him one day, "Ronnie, you could become a great politician—but only if you become a Republican." Big businessmen, he told Ron, were mostly Republicans. They would give lots of money, he said, to an attractive candidate like a popular actor.

June Allyson tried to stop Ronnie one evening during one of his long and sometimes rambling speeches. She asked him a simple question about politics. Ron answered the simple question with a complicated answer. Jane leaned over and whispered to June: "Don't ever ask Ronnie what time it is because he will tell you how a watch is made."

Jane rolled her eyes when Ron "got on his soap box," as a friend once said, to argue politics at parties. "He'll outgrow it," June once told her, laughing.

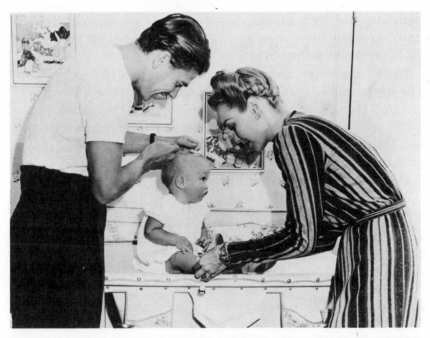

Ron and Jane coiff and dress baby Maureen for a Warner's publicity photo. Movie-fan magazines published photos like this to show readers a "behind-the-scenes" look at the stars. Jane, a friend once said, "in private . . . cared about her home, liked to cook, loved animals, and was (a) loyal friend. Being a film star never changed that."
AUTHOR'S COLLECTION

Jane did not smile. "To her," June once said, "all that talk about politics at every party was no fun."

"Janie always seemed about ten years younger than Ronnie," a friend once said. "She could be the life of the party . . . while he talked about world conditions. He was always very serious. . . ."

Early in 1941, the Reagans became parents, their first child a girl. The baby was christened Maureen Elizabeth. Their two-bedroom apartment near Hollywood Boulevard seemed too small now that they had a baby. An architect designed a large, eight-room house for them perched on a hill high above Sunset Boulevard.

Jane scoured Hollywood buying antique furniture, which she loved, for the new house. Ron reminded her not to "go out on a limb" by spending too much. After *Knute Rockne—All-American*, his pay had shot up to $3,000 a week. But he still feared falling down into the poverty he had escaped.

The Gipper's death scene had not made him an A movie star. The bosses at Warner's liked him because he accepted roles in cheap B movies without complaining. Jimmy Cagney and Bette Davis had refused to play those roles. Warner's knew Cagney and Davis pulled millions into theaters. The studio caved in and gave them juicy roles in A movies. The trusting Ron told people that one day the studio would make him a star.

Jane played even smaller roles, often the silly blond girl friend of the movie's leading lady. "I was never one of those glamour girls," she once said. Since she was sixteen, Jane had seen how studios used contract players, then tossed them aside in favor of younger and prettier or handsomer faces. She worked for the Screen Actors Guild in her spare time, trying to find ways to make the lives of contract players more secure.

A SAG official asked Jane if she would take a seat as an alternate member of SAG's board of directors. Jane would take a seat when another board member could not attend a meeting. She said she was too busy buying furniture and working at their new house, but she brought Ron to the SAG office.

"I don't think you've actually met my husband, Ronald Reagan," she told a SAG official. "But I think he'll make a better alternate than me."

She glanced at Ron with her wide, oval eyes. "A bright light came into her eyes," the official later remembered. She turned back to the official and said, "He might even become president of SAG one day—or maybe America."

Other SAG board members, Jimmy Cagney and Dick Powell among them, happily greeted Ron as an alternate member of the board, which mapped SAG strategy in fighting the studios. Ron soon became one of SAG's most outspoken strategists. "Right from the start," a SAG official said, "he made an impression."

FDR had won the third term. He told Congress that the United States had to help stop the spread of Hitler's Nazi terror across Europe. In the summer of 1941 Hitler plunged into the vastness of Russia. His tanks raced toward Moscow. The troops of his Axis friend, Japan, were conquering China. If Japanese and German armies linked hands, the flags of Germany and Japan would fly over half the globe. America would stand alone, facing the guns of Japan's battleships and the bombers of Hitler's Luftwaffe.

FDR demanded from Congress that America "be prepared." He signed laws that drafted millions of men into the army and navy. He ordered the building of thousands of tanks, war planes, and battleships.

Ron knew he would be called into the army. In Des Moines he had loved riding horses so much he had applied to become a Cavalry officer. The Army made him a second lieutenant in the Reserves—and the Army was now calling up its Reserves.

Warner's asked the Army to wait before asking Ron to go onto active duty. He was making movies, the studio said, that would be costly to stop while it found another actor to play his roles. The Army agreed to postpone calling up Ron.

Late in the summer of 1941 Ron began work on *Kings Row*. It was an A movie about the kind of small towns where Ron had grown up. Ron played Drake McHugh, a playboy women chaser. Of a man like Drake, people said at the time, "he loves 'em and leaves 'em." Ron wasn't the star of *Kings Row*. But when he read the script, he knew he had a scene in which he always did well—a scene which left audiences weeping.

Drake McHugh's legs are injured in an accident. The town's doctor examines him. The doctor believes that Drake has ruined the reputation of his daughter. The doctor knows that Drake's legs could be saved. But he orders that both of Drake's legs be amputated.

Drake awakens from the surgery and looks down at a blanket covering the lower part of his body. He slowly realizes the horror of what has happened to him.

Ron agonized over the scene for weeks. How should a man like Drake react to losing his legs? He talked to surgeons and amputees. In his mind he tried to think like an amputee.

The night before the scene was shot, he couldn't sleep. He came to the set early. No one else was there. He got on the bed and covered his legs with the blanket. He stayed there for an hour. He imagined what it would be like to wake up and suddenly realize he had no legs.

The director came on the set. He saw a look in Ron's eyes and asked, "Want to shoot it?"

"Without rehearsal?" Ron asked, surprised.

"Yes."

Ann Sheridan, a rangy redhead and a good friend of Jane's, played Randy, Drake's girl friend. She stood off-camera so Ron could direct his lines toward her. That would make the scene seem as real as possible for Ron.

The director shouted, "Lights, camera, action!"

The camera zoomed in on Ron as he slowly opened his eyes, looking dazed. His eyes traveled inch by inch down the blanket. Then came a scream that chills late-night-TV-movie audiences to this day:

"Randy! *Where's the rest of me?*"

"There was no retake of that scene," Ron wrote proudly some twenty years later in his autobiography, which he titled, *Where's the Rest of Me?* He added that *Kings Row* "was my best picture."

That scene would vault him into A pictures. But he would never be a star as bright as a Cagney or a Davis. He might have become a star that bright after his appearance in a movie that Warner's planned for him. That 1942 movie made another actor, Humphrey Bogart, forever famous. It was called *Casablanca*. But by then a day in December of 1941 had turned Ronald Reagan, movie actor, into Ronald Reagan, soldier.

In a scene from *Kings Row*, his girl friend Randy (Ann Sheridan) and friend Parris (Robert Cummings) comfort Drake McHugh (Ron) after the amputation of his legs. A few weeks after this scene was shot, Ron went back to Dixon for a preview showing of another movie, *International Squadron*, in which he played a fighter pilot during the 1940 Battle of Britain. Some 30,000 cheered as he and Nelle rode in an open car through the town. His friends waved banners that declared, "Welcome Home Dutch!"
AUTHOR'S COLLECTION

The Soldier

The two Army doctors asked Ron to read the eye chart on the wall. Ron took off his glasses and peered at the wall. He saw a line of wavering black blobs. He tried to read a few lines, guessing at the letters. One doctor stopped him.

"Lieutenant Reagan," the doctor said, "if we sent you overseas, you'd shoot at one of our own generals."

"Yes," said the second doctor, "and you'd miss him."

Ron had entered the Army in April of 1942. Some four months earlier, Japanese planes had bombed the United States Naval base at Pearl Harbor. An angry FDR declared war on Japan and her ally, Hitler's Germany. The United States joined with Great Britain and Soviet Russia to battle Germany and Japan.

His face grim, Ron read newspaper stories that told of American defeats in the Pacific and Russian defeats in Europe. He knew the future of millions of people would be decided by the battles soon to be fought—whether half the world would live in slavery or live free. Hitler had to be defeated.

Ronald Reagan's blurry eyesight took him out of the battles of World War II. As a lieutenant and, later, a captain, he would oversee the making of movies that trained soldiers for those battles.

Ron asked Warner's to pay Nelle a weekly salary since she had no income of her own. He promised to repay the studio

Army Air Corps Lieutenant Ronald Reagan enjoys a night out with his wife at a Hollywood party. Ron resented being called a "chairborne soldier" during World War II. "There was a special job the Army wanted done," he once said of his filmmaking unit. "And it was after men who could do that job." Also serving with the unit at various times were actors Burgess Meredith, Alan Ladd, Clark Gable and Van Johnson. AUTHOR'S COLLECTION

when he went back on salary at war's end. Jack had died a year earlier, felled by a fifth heart attack.

Late in 1942, Warner's decided to make a movie of a Broadway hit musical entitled *This Is the Army*. The movie would star the slim, quick-stepping song-and-dance man, George Murphy, as a showman who whips up a show to help the United States war effort.

Warner's pledged that all profits from the movie would go to American soldiers and their families. The Army let actors like Ron play roles in the film. Ron played Murphy's soldier-son.

George and Ron soon became pals. Murphy had been an FDR Democrat. But he was now a staunch Republican. All during the making of *This Is the Army*, he and Ron argued what Ron liked best—politics. But they stayed good friends.

Ron's new agent was the Music Corporation of America. Nearly all of Hollywood's biggest stars had signed with MCA. If a studio wanted a star for a movie, it had to take two or three of MCA's other actors to get the star. MCA forced the studio bosses to dig into their wallets to pay higher salaries. Early in 1944, Ron signed a contract that would pay him one million dollars for seven years after he made his first post-war movie.

Americans flocked to movies during the war years. They could laugh at comedies and cheer for the Allies in war pictures. At the movies they could forget worries about their men coming home blind, crippled—or not coming home at all.

Many movies were written to give dramatic scenes to women. Jane Wyman began to get some of those good parts. For the first time, movie directors noticed her wide, expressive eyes. In a closeup of those eyes, Jane could show a character's inner emotions without uttering a line.

She got a part playing the girl friend of an alcoholic in *The Lost Weekend*. Her eyes showed her anguish as she saw her lover, played by Ray Milland, staggering along the streets of Manhattan. Milland won an Oscar, movie acting's highest award, for his role in *The Lost Weekend*.

Jane wanted something more than an Oscar—another baby. But she couldn't take time off from making the many movies that were now being offered her. Early in March of 1945, she and Ron adopted a baby boy, naming him Michael. Three-year-old Maureen now had a baby brother.

Ron shuttled each morning from their home in Hollywood to the nearby studio where the training films were made. He came home each evening. But often he came home late, briefcases filled with papers. George Murphy had become president of SAG. He put Ron onto committees to negotiate better contracts for actors. During the filming of *This Is the Army*, said one actress, "Ron would shoot a scene, then rush off somewhere to negotiate. He was a great negotiator."

Jane came home tired from a day's work on a movie set. She wanted to relax with her two babies. Ron wanted to talk into the night about negotiations. Often she nodded off to sleep while he talked.

Early in 1945 FDR suddenly died. "His death," said one friend, "hit Ron hard." Vice President Harry Truman stepped into the White House as the new President. His twangy voice had none of the power and drama of FDR's. Listening to Truman speak on radio one day, Ron turned to a friend and said the speech was "as stirring as mud."

Ron joined the cheering when Truman announced, early in May, that Germany had surrendered and Hitler was dead. Three months later Truman ordered the dropping of the first atomic bomb on Japan—and the Japanese quickly surrendered.

Captain Ronald Reagan became movie actor Ronald Reagan. George Murphy made him a full-time member of SAG's board of directors. Ron took his seat at a table rimmed with some of the world's most famous names and faces: Jimmy Cagney, Robert Montgomery, Henry Fonda, Franchot Tone, Dick Powell, Boris Karloff, Pat O'Brien. Those men—and a handful of women stars—steered SAG through two political storms that blew harder than any in Hollywood's history.

SAG had become part of the gigantic and powerful American Federation of Labor (AFL). Dozens of AFL unions in Hollywood—a carpenters union, an electricians union among them—demanded higher pay for blue-collar workers who built movie sets. The studios said no. The unions voted to strike. And they demanded that SAG join the strike. Without SAG's movie stars, the unions knew, the studios would cave in and give the unions what they wanted.

SAG's board decided not to strike. Most SAG actors and actresses made less than $5,000 a year. If studios stopped making movies, those people would go hungry. Ron agreed with the decision. But the decision split SAG down the middle. FDR Democrats called themselves "liberals." FDR had helped to pick up the working man during the Depression. The liberals wanted to go on helping the union worker.

Other Americans, both Democrat and Republican, called themselves "conservatives." The Great Depression had passed, they said. Now it was time for Americans to stand on their own two feet, with no crutches from the government.

SAG's president named Ron to head an emergency committee

to head off a strike by the blue-collar workers. Ron flew to Chicago and talked face to face with William Green, the AFL's president. As Ron stared aghast, he heard a union leader say there would be a strike and then "there'll be only one man running labor in Hollywood and that man will be me!"

Ron shook his head. Jack and FDR had taught him that unions were the workingman's best friend. But now he saw that a union leader could be just as greedy for power as any studio boss.

He came back to Hollywood and for the first time he wondered: was "old liberal me," as he called himself, right when his heart went out for every cause, like striking with the AFL carpenters? Or were his conservative friends, like Dick Powell and George Murphy, right when they said that the liberals were being tricked by radicals to turn America into a communistic state? No longer was he dead certain that liberals were always right and conservatives always wrong.

SAG's actors did not strike. Angry union workers snarled at Ron. He got anonymous phone calls. One caller snapped, "We'll mess up that pretty face of yours so that you will never work again in front of a camera." For more than six months he carried a gun and slept with it at his side.

The second storm drove a deeper wedge between SAG's liberals and conservatives. By 1947, Americans had come to mistrust their wartime ally, Josef Stalin, and his Communist Russia dictatorship. Some Americans suspected that Stalin had turned his United States Communist Party into a breeding ground for spies and traitors. The Communists, said many Americans, want to turn the United States democracy into a Communist slave state as they did to Poland and Hungary after the war.

A young California lawyer, Richard M. Nixon, campaigned for Congress in 1946. He charged that his Democratic opponent sided too often with the Communists. Nixon won. By the late 1940s, every United States politician knew a candidate had to shout he was anti-Communist—or lose.

One Congressman, New Jersey Democrat J. Parnell Thomas, had made himself famous as a "Red hunter." The short, beefy

Thomas got headlines by claiming that Red spies lurked all over Washington. He got bigger headlines by claiming that Communist actors and writers were turning Hollywood movies into Communist propaganda.

The Federal Bureau of Investigation sent agents to Hollywood to find Communist spies and traitors. Ron told FBI agents that yes, there were Communist party writers and actors in Hollywood. But, he added, there was probably only one Communist among every hundred actors. He agreed to give the FBI the names of any actors he thought were Communist and dangerous. Jane and other liberal friends told Ron that being an informer was wrong.

Studios began to make up "black lists" of actors named as Communists or Communist sympathizers. No studio would hire an actor on that list. Dozens of talented people never again made a living in the movies because of the black list.

J. Parnell Thomas knew he could see his name blazing across front pages if he forced Hollywood stars to testify about Communism in Hollywood. He ordered Ron, George Murphy and Robert Montgomery, then SAG's president, to appear before his committee in Washington. Reporters and fans jammed the committee room to see and hear the stars.

Murphy and Montgomery testified first. Among the committee members was the dark-jowled, husky Congressman from California, Richard Nixon. Both Murphy and Montgomery said they knew of no Communist party traitors or spies in SAG.

Ron sat down to face the committee. "Despite his thirty-six years," a reporter for Newsweek wrote, "the pink-cheeked and sandy-haired Ronald Reagan looked so boyish that when he arose to speak, the room was filled with oohs and aahs."

Ron began his testimony by saying he agreed with Murphy and Montgomery. Then he began to pull a rug out from under the pompous J. Parnell Thomas (who ended up in jail a year later for embezzling funds). In opposing Communism, Reagan said, "the best thing to do is to make democracy work . . . I believe that, as Thomas Jefferson put it, if all the American people know all of the facts, they will never make a mistake."

Ron knew that Thomas wanted to outlaw the Communist

party. "As a citizen," Ron said, "I would hesitate, or not like, to see any political party outlawed on the basis of its political ideology." He said he hated Communism and its tactics. But he added: "I never want to see our country . . . ever compromise with any of our democratic principles through that fear or resentment."

Ron had tiptoed on a tightrope between opposing the Communist party while also putting down those like Thomas who would destroy it. The liberal *New York Times* and the conservative *Life Magazine* both hailed his testimony.

In the midst of the storms around SAG, Ron Reagan tried to make motion pictures. He enjoyed his by-now favorite sport, riding, by galloping on his own horses in the film, *Stallion Road*. But the movie didn't sell a lot of tickets at box offices. He was co-starred with Shirley Temple, the former child actress, in *That Hagen Girl*. The script called for the thirty-six-year-old Ron to fall in love with nineteen-year-old Shirley. A preview audience hooted its disbelief when Ron told Shirley, "I love you!" Sitting in the audience, the red-faced Ron cringed in his seat.

In that picture he had to dive into a river to rescue Shirley. The one-time lifeguard refused to let a stuntman do the rescue. He came down with viral pneumonia, which had killed George Gipp. Jane, at the time, was pregnant. She, too, became ill. She lost the baby. They lay in hospitals miles apart, each too sick to comfort the other.

Jane, meanwhile, had finished her new film, *Johnny Belinda*, in which she played a deaf-mute. In the movie, Jane "talked" by sign language, her ears plugged up with wax so she could not hear. "Jane got as wrapped up in *Johnny Belinda*," a friend said, "as Ron was wrapped up in SAG."

Jane's emotion-filled eyes told weeping audiences of the warmth inside Johnny Belinda—and Jane won an *Oscar* as the best actress of 1948.

June Allyson once said, "her career was going up, his down." Jane and Ron quarreled in public. She told him she was fed up with talk about politics. To a friend she said, "It was exasperating to wake up in the middle of the night, prepare for work, and have someone at the breakfast table, newspaper in hand, expounding on the far right, the far left, the conservative left, and the middle of the road."

In mid-1948 they agreed to divorce. Jane got custody of the two children. They sold their house. Ron kept a small ranch they had bought near Los Angeles where he kept his riding horses. He moved into a small apartment. He dated pretty actresses. But at one party, actress Patricia Neal watched him leave early, tears in his eyes. "It was sad," Neal said, "because he did not want a divorce."

"The problem hurt our children most," Ron later wrote. "There is no easy way to break up a home, and I don't think there is any way to ease the bewildered pain of children at such times."

By 1950 he had made only one worthwhile film since *Kings Row, The Hasty Heart*. And that did only fair at the box office. Playing in a charity softball game, he tripped over actor Eddie Bracken and broke his leg in three places. Stretched out in pain in a hospital bed, he knew his seven-year million dollar contract would soon run out. He also knew that Warner's would not sign him to a new contract. New matinee idols—Marlon Brando, Gregory Peck, Bill Holden—had moved older actors' names off marquees. His movie career seemed to be crumbling. What else could he do besides act?

While Ron twisted and turned in pain in the hospital, bed, a young movie actress was scribbling on a sheet of paper a list of the Hollywood men she would like to marry. First on that list was Ronald Reagan.

The Communicator

The young actress gazed at Ron, her eyes shining with admiration. She and a half-dozen other people were seated around the dining-room table, a maid clearing away the dishes. They listened as Ron talked about how Communist Russia's Josef Stalin wanted to turn all the nations of the world into puppet states that would dance to his tunes. "Tyranny is tyranny," Ron was saying, "whether it comes from the far right"—he meant extreme conservatives—"or from the far left"—he meant extreme liberals or Communists.

Nancy Davis seemed ready to applaud. She had asked a friend to invite her to this dinner party so she could meet Ronald Reagan. Of all the bachelors in Hollywood, he was first on her list of men she wanted to marry.

Nancy was the daughter of Edith Luckett, a stage actress of the 1920s and 1930s. Edith had starred in plays with people who later became movie stars: Pat O'Brien, Spencer Tracy, Zazu Pitts, Walter Huston. She married Ken Robbins, son of a prosperous New England family. Their first and only child, Nancy, was born on July 6, 1921.

Nancy's parents broke up shortly after she was born. While her mother criss-crossed the country with touring stage companies, little Nancy was raised by relatives in Bethesda, Maryland. When Nancy was eight, her mother married Dr. Loyal

Davis, a wealthy Chicago surgeon, Dr. Davis adopted Nancy. She adored the first father she had ever known, often slipping poems she had written under his bedroom door.

Nancy graduated from college in 1943. She decided to be an actress like her mother. "I didn't want to go back to Chicago," she once said, "and live the life of a post-debutante. But I was never a career woman."

Her mother's friend, Zazu Pitts, got her small roles in touring plays. A friend of her father's, singer Mary Martin, got her a part in a Broadway musical. Her mother asked her friend, Spencer Tracy, to help Nancy when he visited New York. Spencer took her out to dinner. Later he called his bachelor pal, Clark Gable, and gave him Nancy's phone number. Visiting New York, Clark dated Nancy several times. But then he went to England where he met and married Lady Sylvia Ashley.

Tracy, meanwhile, asked a friend at Hollywood's Metro-Goldwyn-Mayer studio to give Nancy a screen test. The MGM studio signed Nancy as a contract player. As pretty and petite as a fashion model—she wore size 6 dresses—Nancy appeared in a few small roles. But the role she wanted most was to be the wife of a man as distinguished and strong as her stepfather.

She made friends with Miriam Schary, the wife of MGM executive Dore Schary. She asked Miriam to invite Ron and her, each without a date, to a small dinner party. Miriam said yes. But Ron paid scant attention to the actress who gazed at him starry eyed all evening. Still hobbled by the triple fracture, he had to use a cane to walk. He left early, alone.

Nancy knew how deeply Ron cared about SAG. She phoned him. Could she serve as a replacement on the board when a member had to be absent? Ron asked her out to dinner at a nightclub. Not sure how interesting she would be, he told her he would have to take her home right after dinner because he had an early call at the studio the next morning. She said that was fine. She, too, had an early call. Both were fibbing—there were no early calls for either of them.

At dinner she stared, fascinated, as he talked of political battles within SAG. Nancy hung onto his every word. Ron forgot all about that "early call." Would Nancy like to go to another nightclub? Nancy said fine. She also forgot about her "early call." At 3 A.M. they sat on her doorstep, Ron still talking about the liberal left and the conservative right, Nancy gazing up at him adoringly.

Nancy attended SAG board meetings every other Monday. Before the meetings, she and Ron dined together. She usually said little at the meetings except when she stood to second a motion put to the board by Ron.

Ron dated other actresses. More than once, he said later, he awoke the morning after a date and "I couldn't remember the name of the lady. . . ."

His seven-year Warner's contract had come to an end. He began to make pictures with other studios for $150,000 a picture. He yearned to make a Western. He could ride the horses he loved. By now he had bought a 350-acre ranch high in the California hills. With his own hands he dug posts for the fences of a corral. He hired a trainer for his racing and show horses.

Ron made two westerns—*Cattle Queen of Montana* (the queen was his close friend, Barbara Stanwyck), and *Tennessee's Partner*. Two older actors, Gary Cooper and John Wayne, had stayed popular by playing graying gun-slingers. But audiences never accepted Ron, with his midwestern twang, as a drawling cowboy.

Movie houses across the United States were shutting down. By the mid- 1950s almost one half of American homes sprouted TV antennas from their rooftops. Americans watched old movies on their black-and-white screens. Why pay a dollar to see a movie at a theater when you could see one free at home?

Television had become SAG's Number One enemy. First, TV drew people out of theatres. Secondly, TV showed movies made in the 30s and 40s. The studios sold those movies to TV stations—but the actors who appeared in those movies did not get a dime from the sales to TV. Many were out of work, broke, sometimes hungry. They watched themselves on television screens with growing anger.

Ron was elected president of SAG for a record six straight years. He had to argue with studios. He knew studio bosses probably would not give good parts to an actor they had to argue with day and night.

Ron demanded what were called "residuals" for actors. The studios, he said, should give part of the money to actors when they sold films to TV. The studios refused.

Ron now dated only Nancy. On weekends he took his two growing children, Maureen and Michael, to his ranch. Ron taught the children how to ride horses. He taught Michael how to shoot rifles and pistols. Ron had become a marksman with guns. He was delighted when Maureen and Michael, who lived with Jane Wyman, told him they liked Nancy Davis.

On March 4, 1952, Nancy and Ron were married. They built a four bedroom ranch-style house in Pacific Palisades, not far from Hollywood. From their living room they could look out over the Pacific. Later that year Nancy gave birth to a daughter, Patricia (Patti) Ann.

Ron's movie career kept on sledding downhill. It hit bottom with *Bedtime for Bonzo*. Ron played straight man for the pranks of a chimpanzee named Bonzo. Wrote one critic of Ron and his co-star, Diana Lynne: "Bonzo makes monkeys of them."

Ron still called himself a Democrat. In 1950, Richard Nixon decided to run for the Senate against the Democrats' Helen Gahagan Douglas. Nixon charged that Douglas was a "pinko"— that is, pro-Communist. Ron asked other actors, both Democrats and Republicans, to raise money for Nixon, who beat Douglas and went to the United States Senate.

In 1951 Ron and other Hollywood Democrats sent a telegram to General Dwight D. Eisenhower, who had led Allied troops to victory in Europe in World War II. The telegram asked Ike, as Eisenhower was called, to run for President as a Democrat in 1952.

But Ike chose to run for President as a Republican. His Vice Presidential running mate was Richard Nixon. The Democrats nominated Illinois Governor Adlai Stevenson, a liberal FDR Democrat. Ron voted for Eisenhower and Nixon, who won easily.

Most Americans welcomed the Eisenhower years—1953 to 1960. (Ike and Nixon again beat Stevenson in 1956.) To his millions of supporters, Ike was neither too liberal nor too

conservative. After the turbulence of the past twenty years—
The Great Depression, World War II— Americans were grateful
for the serene 1950s. Ike ended a war in Korea that had killed
thousands of American GIs battling Communist North Korea
and Communist China.

Stock-market prices soared, houses rose in value, and the
neatly- manicured green lawns and tree-lined streets of suburbs popped up around big cities. But slum areas of those cities
turned into ghettos filled with the fearful poor: blacks and
Hispanics stalked by drug addicts, robbers and killers. Millions
of these poor had no skills. Without jobs, they lived on money—
"welfare"—from the city or state. Year by year, the cost of
welfare—and the millions living on welfare—swelled in number.

Poor blacks demanded better schools for their kids. The US
Supreme Court ruled that kids in all-black schools must be
allowed to enter better equipped all-white schools. Ghetto kids
were taken by buses to all-white neighborhoods to go to school.
Liberals applauded the busing of kids to integrated schools.
Many conservatives said busing was wrong and that kids
should go to their neighborhood's schools. Busing and the
integration of schools and neighborhoods, said conservatives,
destroyed the right of Americans to choose their own neighbors.

Ron had twice voted for Ike. But he told people he still
considered himself a Democrat. He had become a conservative
Democrat. He told friends that he opposed soaring income
taxes and a ballooning federal payroll. Government agencies,
he argued, wasted money on low-rent housing projects and
other programs that were supposed to help the poor but did
not.

"It's time to get the government out of our wallets," he told
people. Yes, he said, government had helped people during The
Great Depression. "But what was a helping hand," he said, "has
now become a steel fist."

In 1954 the General Electric Company sent officials to talk to
Ron. The electric giant wanted to sponsor a TV show, the
General Electric Theatre. Ron would be its host. He would

introduce the star of each week's show—movie stars like Bob Hope. Ron would also star in several shows.

That was half of his job for G.E., at a salary of $150,000 a year. The other half: G.E. wanted Ron to visit its 135 plants scattered across the country. They wanted Ron to talk to their 700,000 employees and let them know that the company cared about them.

The G.E. Theatre shot high in the ratings to become one of the nation's most popular TV shows. And Ron walked the floors of G.E. plants from coast to coast.

"He communicated on the level of the working man and woman," a G.E. official said of the man who would later be called The Great Communicator. Women crowded around him, begging for autographs, even slipping him love notes.

The men kept their distance. Some threw nasty remarks toward Ron concerning the manliness of movie actors.

Ron talked to the women. Then he strolled over to the men. He talked about a recent football or baseball game. He dropped the names of sports heroes he knew. He told jokes that drew belly laughs. The men asked questions about their labor union and G.E.'s rules.

Ron told them quickly that he was a union man himself. Then he answered their questions in a simple, direct way. "When he left them ten minutes later," a G.E. official said, "they were slapping him on the back and saying, 'That's the way, Ron.' "

He visited plants from dawn to near midnight, slept at a hotel, then rushed off by train the next morning to another plant. During these ten-week tours, he worked seven days a week.

Often he spoke at luncheons to local groups of businessmen or lawyers. He insisted on writing his own speeches even though G.E. offered him speech writers. A teacher once asked him to speak to her group which would meet thirty minutes later.

"Don't do it," a G.E. official said. "What do you know about education?"

"Don't worry," Ron said.

He sat down and scribbled a speech "in that crabbed handwriting of his which is hard to read," the official said. "Then he got up there and gave a speech on education that just dropped them in the aisles. He got standing applause . . . This is when I finally began to realize the breadth of his knowledge . . . everything that went into that mind stayed there."

Ron was learning how to campaign. He was doing what all politicians must do to win—talking face to face with people, shaking hands, what politicians call "pressing the flesh."

In 1956 Ron had resigned as SAG's president. SAG continued to battle the movie studios for money from the sale of movies to TV stations. By 1959, SAG had decided to strike for the money. SAG officials asked Ron to come back as president. "We wanted a strong leader," a SAG official said, "and everybody's mind turned back to Ronnie Reagan."

Nancy begged him to refuse. The job would take time away from his G.E. tours. No movie roles were coming his way. And now he and Nancy had a second child, Ronald Reagan, Jr., born in 1958. He shared with Jane Wyman the high cost of private schools for Maureen and Michael. And the ranch and its horses had nibbled into his savings.

But he said "yes" to actors he could not walk away from during a strike. The strike dragged on. Ron met with the studio bosses. One boss said to him, "You know, Ronnie, if we give you the TV money, we will then be asked by the actors to pay residuals when we re-issue old movies to theatres."

Ron sniffed a change in the wind. The studios, he sensed, would give the TV money in return for a guarantee that they would not have to pay money when they re-issued old films.

"Paying the actors for re-issuing old movies is something that will never happen—not in our lifetimes," Ron said.

That swayed the studios. They set up a two million dollar fund for actors, to pay for movies already sold to TV. And from then on every SAG actor got money for movies sold to TV.

Ron had learned how to make a deal. "The trick," he once said, "is to find out the most the other side is willing to give. Then you decide how much you are willing to give up to get that 'most' from the other side."

In 1960 the Republicans nominated Richard Nixon to run

Ron and Nancy pose for a publicity portrait for *Hellcats of the Navy*, a 1957 movie and the only one they made together. In the movie he played a submarine commander, she a nurse. Ron had a fear of closed places. As a result, he would not fly in a plane for years. Locked in a cramped sub for hours during the shooting of *Hellcats*, he dreaded each day's shooting. The need to fly during election campaigns finally erased his fear of flying.
COURTESY REAGAN PRESIDENTIAL MATERIALS STAFF

against the Democrats' John F. Kennedy for the Presidency. A liberal Democrat, Kennedy's handsome face, vibrant voice and challenging speeches brought back memories of FDR to millions of Democrats, both liberal and conservative. Kennedy won.

Ron voted for Nixon but still called himself a Democrat. By now newspapers had labeled Ron "a prominent conservative spokesman for General Electric." Ron did not object to being called a conservative. To Ron, a conservative meant being opposed to Communists taking over the nation and the world. And if being a conservative meant being against a big and bossy government in Washington, Ron said, "Call me a conservative."

Touring for G.E., Ron often voiced fears that the Communists would make America "a slave state by 1970." One union newspaper accused him of being an "extremist."

"I've been making this same speech for years and no one objected," Ron snapped. "Then a Democratic President is elected and suddenly they find I'm an . . . extremist." An angry Ron switched parties and officially became a Republican.

In 1964, the Republicans nominated Arizona Senator Barry Goldwater to run against Lyndon B. Johnson, who had become President after the assassination of John Kennedy. By now American soldiers were fighting a communist-led army in Viet Nam. Goldwater called for America to destroy world communism. Johnson told the nation that Goldwater would start an atomic war.

Ron made a speech on national television for Goldwater. Millions listened as Ron said that Americans must choose between war and "saying to a billion human beings now in slavery behind the Iron Curtain, 'Give up your dreams of freedom because to save our own skin we are willing to make a deal with your taskmasters.' "

And he concluded with words borrowed from FDR:

"You and I have a rendezvous with destiny. We can reserve for our children this last best hope of man on earth, or we can sentence them to take their first steps into a thousand years of darkness."

Nancy and Ron share a Christmas in the mid-1960s (l. to r.): Michael, Ron, Jr., and Patti. Michael was never able to conceal his jealousy of Ron, Jr., because Ron had been named after his father. Maureen and Patti, poles apart politically, were never close as sisters. For years Michael had to be careful not to pose for newspaper pictures with Nancy. The pictures upset his mother, Jane Wyman.
COURTESY REAGAN PRESIDENTIAL MATERIALS STAFF

Goldwater lost. But conservatives, both Democrats and Republicans, smiled when they recalled that speech by Ron. His handsome, tanned face and electric-blue eyes seemed to jump off TV screens into living rooms. He came across on TV as everybody's best friend. Politicians had suddenly become aware that to win a Presidency, a candidate had to appear on TV as a winning, good kind of person.

"I don't think he's the most brilliant man I ever met," one wealthy Republican said. "But I always knew Ron was a real leader. . . . He can get on his feet and influence people."

A group of wealthy California Republicans asked Ron to run for Governor of the state in 1966. They chipped in almost half a million dollars to pay for the campaign.

Maureen Reagan now worked in Washington as a secretary. She loved politics. She wrote to her father and urged him to run. She told him he would make a great Governor.

"Well, if we're talking about what I could do," he wrote back in a joshing way, "I could be President."

The Governor

"Ronnie Reagan is just an actor," Governor Pat Brown's assistant said to the governor. "We'll beat him easily."

The owlish-faced, Democrat governor nodded. Pat Brown had governed California for eight years. Now, in 1966, he could point to picture-postcard state parks, some of the nation's best high schools and colleges, and a superb highway system. Brown had backed President Lyndon Johnson's civil rights laws and the president's war on poverty. That had won him the cheers of liberals. In his campaign speeches, Brown boasted how he had made California great. Then he added as audiences laughed: "And while I helped to do all that, my opponent was making *Bedtime for Bonzo!*"

Brown landed heavier punches on Ron when he told audiences that Ron was no friend to the poor and blacks. Ron had opposed civil rights laws of the early 1960s, which opened the doors of all-white neighborhoods and schools to blacks and other minorities. Ron said the constitution gave every citizen the right to rent a house to any person—and if you didn't want to rent your home to a certain person, that was your right too. Then Ron added: "I've spent my life opposing racism and bigotry. My record proves it."

Ron said that Lyndon Johnson's war on poverty only made the poor poorer. Welfare checks, he said, were only crutches.

Welfare kept people hobbling in poverty, people who should be given paid jobs so they could walk on their own.

Most California voters were Democrats. Ron told Democrats that FDR had helped the "forgotten man"—the man or woman at the bottom of the heap during the Depression. Now, said Ron, that person had risen to the middle of the heap. That person worked fifty to sixty hours a week, lived in the suburbs, hoped to pay his kids' way through college, "but is being taxed and taxed for the benefit of someone else." Ron told cheering middle-class voters that he wanted to help that new "forgotten American."

Both Democrats and Republicans nodded thoughtfully when Ron told them that welfare costs were skyrocketing taxes. Ron ended his speech with the words: "Had enough?"

Audiences roared back a resounding "yes!" Ron buried Pat Brown under an avalanche of votes, winning 3.7 million to Brown's 2.7 million. One of Brown's aides said of Ron's victory: "Part of what happened is that we put him down as an actor in a state where actors are idols. But the roots of our mistake go deeper. Reagan is terribly pleasant, highly articulate, and has a serious approach to politics . . . People like him, and we didn't understand that."

After being sworn in as governor early in 1967, Ron read from a speech he had written: "For many years now, you and I have been shushed like children and told there are no simple answers to the complex problems which are beyond our comprehension. Well, the truth is that there are simple answers—there are just no easy ones."

Ron's simple—but not easy—answer: The state should not spend more money than it takes in. In short, it should balance its budget. And he threw out a challenge that would be the watchword of his eight years as governor:

"We are going to squeeze and cut and trim until we reduce the cost of government."

Quickly he showed how he could communicate complex concepts to the man in the street by using short, colorful quotes that put him on TV and the front pages. "The symbol of our state flag is the Golden Bear," he told reporters. "It is not a cow to be milked."

He hired business executives to run state agencies. One, Caspar W. (Cap) Weinberger, managed the agency that made sure the state did not spend more money than it took back in taxes. A public relations executive, Mike Deaver, gave Ron advice on how to get favorable stories in the newspapers and on TV.

Cap and Mike knew that Ron did not yet understand how the intricate machinery of state government and politics really worked. They advised Ron to say, "I don't know" when reporters asked him a question he couldn't answer. "Better to say you don't know than give the wrong answer," Cap told him. "Wrong answers end up as nasty headlines."

But Ron, new to elected office, had a lot to learn about how to run a state of more than sixteen million people. He made mistakes. When reporters pointed out the mistakes, Ron flashed his still-boyish smile, shrugged and said, "I goofed."

Reporters liked him. He may not know much, they said, but he didn't try to cover up his mistakes like most politicians.

As the governor, Ron looked upon himself as a general commanding an army. The general decides what goals his army should reach and how they should fight to reach those goals. The general then tells his colonels to lead their troops so that they fight day by day toward those goals. Ron's colonels were the men and women directing agencies in charge of schools, housing, highways, police and other services provided by the state.

His critics sneered that Ron used "colonels" because the ex-actor didn't know how to run the state's agencies. Ron's admirers replied: No governor should get snarled up in the day-to-day running of an agency. A governor must stand watch over the complete picture. And if he or she sees that one agency is stumbling, the governor gets a new chief who makes that agency run as it should.

Ron and Nancy lived in a mansion in Sacramento, the capital of California. A chauffeur driven car took him to the governor's office at 9 each morning. He worked until 5 P.M. Driven home, he swam in his backyard pool with ten-year-old Ron, Jr., whom he called Skipper. Sixteen-year-old Patti lived away from home at a private school for girls.

After supper—meat and potatoes or macaroni and cheese were Ron's favorites—Ron watched TV in his bedroom, often stretched out on the bed. His favorite shows were *Mission Impossible* and another suspense show, *Mannix*. His favorite performers were comedienne Carol Burnett and singer Dean Martin. On weekends he watched pro football and rooted for his favorite team, the Los Angeles Rams.

He and Nancy fled Sacramento on weekends and drove to their Pacific Palisades home. Or they drove to the ranch. Ron had swapped his ranch in the hills for a 688-acre spread high above the ocean near Santa Barbara. Ron called it his "heavenly ranch." He and Nancy lived in a Spanish-style house. Ron and Skipper rode the ranch's Arabian horses.

The twenty-three-year-old Michael sometimes came to visit his father. He had dropped out of school and worked as a boat salesman. He now resented Nancy and thought she disliked him. Nancy scolded Michael because, she said, he made Ron worry. Michael and Maureen, who worked in Washington, called Nancy "the Dragon Lady," the name of a comic-strip villainess.

Nancy and Jane Wyman detested each other. Nancy would not allow Jane's name to be mentioned in any official biography of Ron. Jane was made to feel that Ron never had a first wife. Nancy thought that Jane had not raised Maureen and Michael properly. With the two women hissing at each other from afar, a glacier grew between Jane's two children, Maureen and Michael, and Nancy's two, Patti and Ron, Jr.

Sixteen-year-old Patti yearned to be an actress like her mother and grandmother. She inherited her grandfather Jack's fiery liberalism and from her grandmother the concern for the unfortunate. (Nelle had died in a nursing home in 1962.) She muttered angrily when her father spoke out against Lyndon Johnson's war on poverty. She screamed at her father when he spoke to support LBJ's war against Communist North Viet Nam. Like many students of the 1960s, Patti wanted America to get out of the war. She joined campus demonstrations. Bearded young man and long-haired young women flaunted banners that shrieked, "Hey, hey, LBJ, how many men have you killed today?"

Patti's face turned crimson when campus protesters pointed her out as Governor Reagan's daughter, Patti began to call herself Patti Davis. That angered Nancy. Mother and daughter drifted wider apart.

"He was the protected one and she was the protector," newspaperman Lou Cannon once wrote of Ron and Nancy. When anyone said or did anything that might hurt Ronnie, as she called him (he called her "Mommy"), Nancy's wrath fell like a ton of bricks on the offender. If an aide made a mistake that made Ron look foolish to the public, Nancy demanded the aide be fired. When her slight figure sailed into the governor's office, nearly always dressed in her favorite color—red—the faces of assistants turned pale. Behind her back they called her "The Iron Maiden."

"During a campaign," a Reagan aide once said of Nancy, "I had her going morning, noon and night. She never complained. But if she heard that Ron had to get up at 6 A.M. for a TV show, she'd scream bloody murder because she always wanted him to get his rest."

When Ron made a speech, Nancy stood nearby and stared upward at him with a fixed, adoring look. Reporters dubbed the look 'The Gaze.' "She loves him so much that she doesn't have to put on that phony look," a friend once said. "She was an actress, but she doesn't realize that 'The Gaze,' which is an act, isn't good acting."

A reporter once asked Nancy if she had ever thought of life without Ronnie. "Never!" she replied quickly. "Oh! The thought of it would terrify me . . . You see, he's a rare man. When we first came to Sacramento, there were comments that he was kind of snobby, that he didn't stay after hours to have drinks with the men. Well, it was that way in the picture business. After a day's shooting, he didn't go out with the other men. He always wanted to come home. And I don't go off by myself either."

Lou Cannon once asked Ron what Nancy meant to him. "How

do you describe coming into a warm room out of the cold?"
Ron replied. "Never waking up bored? The only thing wrong is,
she's made a coward out of me. Whenever she's out of my sight,
I'm worried about her."

Mike Deaver, one of the few Reagan aides who was close to
Nancy, once said of her: "Nancy Reagan spent a good deal of her
time in life making a good life for Ronald Reagan, making sure
he was comfortable, making sure things were done right . . . I
don't think she's gotten credit for that. She was as much
responsible for his success as he is."

As California's governor, Ron would fight two major battles to
keep his promise about not spending more money than the
state took in. Students at state-supported colleges paid no
tuition. Ron demanded they pay up to $300 a year.

Students organized marches and demonstrations to protest
the tuition. They tore up offices, scribbled four-letter words on
walls, even burned American flags.

A speech by Dutch Reagan had sparked one of the first
campus strikes. But at Eureka, he told aides, "we didn't rip and
tear and destroy. Our only weapons were words."

An angry Governor Reagan went on TV. "Classes have been
disrupted," he said. "Property has been destroyed." Ron ordered state police to chase strikers off campuses.

Students fought back. Hundreds were hurt, one killed. Ron
remembered his SAG negotiating days. He began to work behind
the scenes.

After conferring with university officials, he agreed to con-
tinue what was sacred to students—"free tuition." But he got
the officials to agree to a $200 "charge" to be paid by all
students. "Call it a 'charge' or call it 'tuition,' " a Reagan aide
said, "but the governor won the battle."

His second battle was to cut the cost of feeding what he called
"The Welfare Monster." The state, he said, couldn't pay to
improve schools and highways because so much money was
being paid to what he called "welfare cheats." These were
people, he charged, too lazy to work or who got cash for their

Governor Reagan goes to work in Sacramento. He accepted the nomination to run with reluctance. His brother, Moon, a Los Angeles advertising executive, convinced him he had to make a name for himself as Governor of California before going for the "big one."
COURTESY OF CALIFORNIA STATE ARCHIVES

work while also collecting welfare. The cheaters, he said, got money that should have gone to "the truely needy."

Ron had been reelected in 1970 to a second term. But he had learned that his popularity with voters did not always give him the muscle to get his ideas passed into laws.

He sat down with the leader of the Democratic law makers, the politically smart, brash Bob Moretti. "Look, governor," Moretti growled. "I don't like you particularly well, and I know you don't like me. But we don't have to be in love to work together. If you're serious about doing something, let's do it."

Ron and Moretti created the California Welfare Reform Act. People on welfare dropped from 1.6 million to 1.3 million, a saving of $2 billion. And payments to those who needed help jumped by almost fifty percent. "By almost any yardstick— liberal, conservative, managerial," Lou Cannon wrote, "the law has been a success."

In 1974 Ron decided not to seek a third term even though he had become the most popular politician in the state. Two of every three voters said he had been a success as governor. Of Reagan, Moretti said: "He had an enduring desire to leave something behind that was really material which he could point to as a change. He wanted to improve where he had been."

By 1974 the Republican party had sunk to its lowest popularity level in one hundred years. In 1968 Richard Nixon had won the presidency, defeating the Democrats' Hubert Humphrey. The war in Viet Nam had ended with America's defeat. But Nixon won applause from liberals and conservatives by visiting Communist China. Hopes for peace between the western democracies and world communism seemed the brightest since the Cold War began. In 1972 Nixon easily won re-election.

Then came the Watergate scandal. Republican officials, perhaps involving the President, had sent burglars to ransack the headquarters of the Democrats. Nixon had to resign, succeeded by Vice President Gerald Ford.

Could Ford win the Presidency for the Republicans in 1976? Few experts thought so. By 1975 only eighteen percent of Americans called themselves Republicans. Wealthy Californians asked Ron to run as a third-party candidate against Ford and the Democrats. He refused. "I do not believe the Republican party is dead," he said. Most Americans, he added, believed what the Grand Old Party believed—"getting big government off their backs." He told the G.O.P.: "We can get that message across to people. I am going to try to do that."

In the winter and spring of 1976, Ron campaigned across the country to win the G.O.P. nomination to run as President. He entered state primary elections to try to win delegates to the G.O.P.'s national convention. He was campaigning against Gerald Ford, the President of the United States, and the might of that office. Yet Ron got 1,070 delegates to vote for him at the convention, only about a hundred fewer than the 1,187 for Ford, who won the G.O.P. nomination.

Nancy wept as Ron told the convention delegates: "Recognize that there are millions and millions of Americans out there that want what you want . . . (an America) that is a shining city on a hill."

Later he comforted Nancy with lines from an English ballad that he had memorized as a boy:

"Though I am wounded, I am not slain. I shall rise and fight again."

The Candidate

Ron laughed as Dustin Hoffman snapped off a funny remark at his ex-wife, played by Meryl Streep. He was watching a new movie, *Kramer vs. Kramer,* in the home of Hollywood producer Hal Wallis late in the winter of 1980.

The screen suddenly flashed white. A voice cut across the darkened room. "Sorry," said the man who had stopped the movie. "There's an important call for Mr. Reagan from Iowa."

Ron jumped from his chair. He dashed to the phone. A few hours earlier, the polls had closed in Iowa. Republicans in that state were picking delegates to the 1980 G.O.P. convention. During the past four years since narrowly losing the nomination to Gerald Ford, Ron had crisscrossed the nation trying to win delegates to that 1980 convention.

Ron picked up the phone. An aide in Iowa City began to rattle off numbers. George Bush had won with thirty-three percent of the votes. Ron had received thirty percent.

"It was a jolt," Ron said later. As he hung up the phone, he thought to himself: I haven't been this low since I lost that Montgomery Ward job in Dixon almost fifty years ago.

Now almost sixty-nine years old, Ron would be seventy-one if he were sworn in as President in 1981. The oldest President, William Henry Harrison, had been sixty-nine, and had died in office. Ron knew that 1980 was his last chance to be President.

Lots of people were saying even in 1980 that he was too old to be President.

Ron put down the telephone. He turned to an assistant and said grimly, "There are going to be some changes made."

Although Gerald Ford had won the G.O.P. nomination in 1976, he'd lost the Presidency to Jimmy Carter, a liberal Democrat who had been governor of Georgia. At first most Americans liked the fair-haired Carter. He seemed to care for the the poor, the working man and woman, as well as blacks and other minorities. Many Americans thought that Nixon and Ford had care more for "the big guys," meaning giant corporations. It was good, some people said, that now there was a man in the White House who cared for "the little guy."

But by 1979 events at home and overseas had made many of Carter's supporters wonder about him. In 1979 Russian troops invaded neighboring Afghanistan. Afghanistani men, women and children fought the Russian tanks with hand-made rifles. To protest the invasion, Carter said that American athletes would not compete in Moscow in the 1980 Olympic Games. "What's the Olympics got to do with our foreign policy?" disappointed Americans complained.

Later in 1979, Iranian revolutionaries seized more than fifty Americans in Teheran, the nation's capital. The revolutionaries were supported by their dictatorship government. The rebels said they would hold the Americans hostages until Carter sent the former ruler of Iran, the Shah, back to Teheran for trial and execution. The Shah was being treated for cancer in New York. Carter refused.

Instead he sent helicopters to try to swoop into Teheran and free the hostages. The helicopters broke down in the Iranian desert and had to be destroyed. If the commander-in-chief's helicopters broke down like old jalopies, Americans said, how good were his planes, tanks and battleships?

At home "sticker shock" became a new phrase among consumers. The shock came when buyers looked at the prices on the stickers of cars, refrigerators and other expensive products.

The price of a car had doubled in a few years. But people were being paid the same salaries they had earned a few years earlier.

Economists said America had been stricken by "stag-flation." What that meant was: prices shot up while income stayed stagnant.

Carter conceded that the country was sick. On national television he said the nation had been dragged down by a "crisis of confidence . . . that strikes at the very heart and soul of our national will." Others called the crisis a "malaise," a sickness like the flu that makes a person slow and apathetic. Many Americans began to blame Carter and other liberal Democrats for the stag-flation. Taxes had gone up while billions were being spent on welfare as part of Carter's and Lyndon Johnson's "war on poverty."

In speech after speech, Ron Reagan told how he would make America well. He would spend less money on welfare, education, health research and other liberal programs. They were good programs, he said, but billions were being wasted by the program's bureaucrats. He would cut taxes. That would put more money in people's pockets. They could spend to buy products. Then factories would start to hum again. And he would spend more money to build up our defenses so America's helicopters wouldn't break down, among other things. Terrorists, still holding American hostages, wouldn't be able to thumb their noses at Uncle Sam.

Reagan's economics would soon be called Reaganomics. His speeches made sense to many Americans concerned about stag-flation, but liberal Republicans argued that Reaganomics made no sense. One of those was George Bush, a tall, slim World War II hero. He had been a Republican Congressman from Texas and the director of the Central Intelligence Agency. Bush lashed out at Reaganomics, saying that "you can't cut taxes and raise defense spending." Scornfully, he called Reaganomics "Voodoo Economics."

Ron led Bush in most polls of Republicans across the country. Ron's advisers told him not to debate Bush head to head. Ron could still spew out facts, which he memorized by reading bundles of newspapers and magazines each week. He could talk about the costs of an engine in a B-1 bomber or how a woman in a small Missouri town got $200 a month in welfare checks while she had a bank account worth $3 million.

But sometimes his photographic memory mixed up his facts. Or he'd tell an anecdote about a welfare cheat and then learn, red-faced, that the cheat had been made up by an imaginative newspaper reporter.

Ron wanted to debate Bush. But he went along with the advice of aides, who said, "You're way ahead of Bush in the polls. Don't say the wrong thing in a debate that would give Bush a lift."

But now, defeated in Iowa, Ron said he would stand up to Bush and say what he thought was right for the nation. "A team doesn't win the Super Bowl if its best passer sits on the bench," Ron told his aides. "I sat on my behind in Iowa."

He rushed off to New Hampshire, site of the next Republican primary. Riding in a bus, he shot around the cold, snowy state for twenty-one straight days. Some voters had thought Ron was too old to campaign. Reporters had joked about the Ron Reagan doll: "You wind it up and it runs for an hour and then takes a nap." But after New Hampshire, as thirty-year-old reporters panted to keep up with Ron, few people thought Ron too old to be President.

Ron dared Bush to debate him on live TV. Bush said yes, but only if he and Ron debated one-on-one. Four other Republicans were also running for the nomination in New Hampshire. Ron said they should also be allowed to debate. A date was set, the debate to be held in a school gym in Nashua. Bush kept insisting he would debate only Ron.

Ron said he would pay for the cost of the debate. Ron and the four other candidates arrived at the crowded gym. TV lights glared. Ron saw Bush sitting alone on the stage. Bush's aides told Ron that he would debate only Ron.

Ron heard a Nashua editor begin to explain to the crowd, packed in the gym, that the rules allowed only a debate between Ron and Bush.

Ron strode to the stage. The four other candidates followed him. Ron's aides stared, not knowing what he would do next. He grabbed a microphone.

"Turn Mr. Reagan's microphone off," the editor ordered.

"I paid for this microphone, Mr. Green," Ron snapped. Fury shone in his eyes. The crowd cheered. Bush still sat stiffly, looking like a small boy dropped off, someone said later, "at the wrong birthday party."

Millions saw that scene the next day on their TV screens. A reporter for The Boston Globe wrote, "At a high school in Nashua, the Gipper grabbed the brass ring." Ron easily won the New Hampshire primary. A few months later Bush dropped out of the race.

His biographer, Lou Cannon, once compared Ron to a lazy football player who is suddenly hit illegally from behind. Enraged, the player then terrorizes anything that comes into his path. "Reagan is like that," Cannon wrote, "He is no menace . . . when left alone, but a fury when aroused."

The Republicans gathered in Detroit to pick their nominees for President and Vice President. With the first vote they unanimously chose Ron to be the nominee for President. Everyone wondered: who would be Ron's choice to run with him as vice president?

George Bush had angered Ron in New Hampshire. But Ron knew that the G.O.P. ticket would be better balanced with Bush, more liberal than Ron, running as Vice President. Ron asked the delegates to select Bush as Vice President—and they agreed.

Then Ron surprised the Republican delegates. He began to praise a Democrat, the liberal who was his first political hero— FDR. He said that FDR had lifted up a sick nation and made it healthy. The former lifeguard said he would try to be a president like FDR and pull the nation out of disasters at home and overseas.

The Democrats nominated Jimmy Carter to try for a second term. Ron and Carter agreed to a live debate on national television.

"Stay relaxed," Mike Deaver told him. But Deaver worried that Ron might lose the debate. He worried that Ron might seem afraid of Carter. "Ron always thought a president stood ten feet tall," Deaver later said.

Ron seemed nervous as the debate began. He stumbled over answers. But when he talked about the "wasteful spending" of the Carter years, he saw Carter stiffen and glare at him.

The subject turned to Medicare for the aged and needy. Carter's anger pushed him into a mistake. "Governor Reagan, as a matter of fact," he said, "began his political career campaigning around the country against Medicare."

That was not true. Ron let Carter finish. Then he seemed to sigh as though asking himself, "What am I going to do about this mixed-up child?"

He turned to Carter and said in a pitying tone, "There you go again." At home, millions laughed. He had made Carter look like a child who had once again made the same silly mistake. Aides had filled Ron's heads with hundreds of facts, but that simple "there you go again" made Carter look five feet tall.

Ron finished another debate by asking Americans "this basic question": "Are you happier today than when Mr. Carter became President of the United States?"

Most Americans answered "No!" Ron won easily with almost 44 million votes to 35.4 million for Carter.

As the returns poured into his hotel suite in Los Angeles, Ron hugged Nancy. His brother Moon arrived and shouted across the laughter and shouting, "I bet there's a hot time in Dixon tonight."

"I'd like to be there off in a corner just listening," said President-elect Ronald Reagan.

Early in March of 1981 he took the oath of office. Nancy stood beside him, the gaze still loving. Sitting nearby were his four children. His oldest daughter, Maureen, had campaigned for him with her brother, Mike. Both were now married and Mike had presented the new President with his first grandchild, a boy. Patti and Ronald, Jr., sat near each other, but kept their distance from Maureen and Mike, Jane Wyman's two children. Greetings were polite but cool.

Maureen was now almost forty. She had bounced back from two divorces to find a happy married life and a career as a campaign strategist and speech writer for the Republican national committee.

The new President locks hands to show cheering crowds at his 1981 inaugural parade that he is the champion. The new First Lady gives a lady-like wave. Nancy immediately began to redecorate the White House with the expensive elegance of Jackie Kennedy, whisking away the more austere styles and furnishings favored by the Carters, Fords, Nixons and Johnsons.
COURTESY REAGAN PRESIDENTIAL MATERIALS STAFF

Mike, now thirty-five, had been a speedboat racer—he won several championships—and a salesman. He dreaded seeing himself described as "the adopted son" of Jane Wyman and President Reagan. He told friends that he felt "like an outsider looking in" at the first family. He was often broke, borrowing money from his father. Amid the pomp of the swearing in, he wondered where he could get a job. And he hid a secret from his father. He feared if his father found out about that secret, his father would no longer love him.

Patti, now twenty-eight, had lived with a rock 'n' roll singer, angering her parents. But now she told them that she would soon marry—and she did. She lived in California and seldom visited her father because she would argue with him that he was taking food and shelter from the poor. She wanted to be an actress, and she had also begun to work on a book about the family.

The youngest, Ron, Jr., was now twenty-three. Like Mike, he wondered where he could get a job. He told friends he would like to be a ballet dancer. He knew his father and mother thought male ballet dancers were effeminate and likely to be homosexual.

All four of the children loved Ron. They competed with each other for his attention. As teenagers, all had been jealous of Nancy because they felt their father listened to her and not to them. But with the exception of Patti, they had come closer to Nancy because of her love for their father. They shared one resentment: having to phone Mike Deaver or some other aide when they wanted to talk to their father. They understood a President is busy, but this was their father. When they got through to Dad, as they called him, he listened patiently to their problems and gave them advice. But Ron had never lav-

Members of the Reagan family and their in-laws gather around the new President and his First Lady at the 1981 Inaugural, Nancy wearing her inaugural gown. From left to right: Anne and Geoffrey Davis, Maureen Reagan Revell and her husband Dennis, Colleen and Michael Reagan and their son Cameron, Bess and Neil (Moon) Reagan, Patricia and Richard Davis, Patti Reagan, and Doria and Ronald Reagan, Jr.
COURTESY REAGAN PRESIDENTIAL MATERIALS STAFF

ished expensive gifts on his children. A check for fifty dollars was a usual birthday gift.

Striding into the Oval Office for his first day of work, Ron arrived at 9 A.M. and made it clear he would go back upstairs to Nancy and his family promptly at 5 P.M. He knew that Presidents Carter, Nixon and Johnson often stayed at work until after midnight. Ron didn't think a President should be buried under an avalanche of paper-work details. His aides could handle the details while the President looked at "the big picture." He told Deaver, "Show me an executive who works long overtime hours, and I'll show you a bad executive."

The burdens of the Presidency had visibly aged Carter and Johnson. President Reagan said he wanted to enjoy the Presidency. The press secretary to President Kennedy, Pierre Salinger, said both men took office with the same easy-going way. "Kennedy," he said, "like Reagan, didn't seem to be overburdened by being President and he didn't take himself too seriously."

Reagan's three closest advisors were Mike Deaver and Ed Meese, his two trusted California lieutenants, and a Texas lawyer, James Baker, who was Chief of Staff. Reporters called Baker, Meese and Deaver the Triumvirate. The trio were the most powerful men in Washington. They gave orders that carried all the power of an order from the President.

The tall, broad-chested Baker had managed the Presidential campaigns of Gerald Ford in 1976, and George Bush in 1980. By now he knew every important politician in the nation. As Reagan's Chief of Staff, he bossed the White House—but his Number One job was to line up Congressmen and Senators to vote for the bills that the President wanted passed into law.

The burly, big-fisted Meese, an Army Reserve Lieutenant Colonel, made sure that the President's orders were carried out by the hundreds of "soldiers" in the White House. If the President ordered money to go to victims of a hurricane, Meese's line of command passed down the order until it was obeyed. Meese also wrote out the President's daily schedule, one that Ron followed to the minute. If an ambassador was scheduled to visit the President at 9:35, Ron liked to have his desk—and his mind—cleared so that at 9:35 he was thinking only of what he wanted to say to the ambassador.

The balding, bustling Mike Deaver even made cabinet officers worry. The reason: orders from Nancy came directly from her to Deaver, who made sure the orders were carried out—or else. The Reagans both looked upon him almost like a favorite child, angering Maureen and Michael. He was a publicity man who created what are called "images"—making people appear to be what they may or may not really be like. Deaver devoted himself to making Ron and Nancy always shine whenever they appeared in public.

The 40th President insisted that his administration make good on his campaign promises. He had promised American farmers that he would allow them to sell grain to Russia. President Carter had stopped the sales after the invasion of Afghanistan. Secretary of State Alexander Haig protested lifting the ban.

"Lift the ban," Ron said. "I promised to do it, Al."

During the campaign Reagan had said he would consider naming the first woman to the Supreme Court. When a seat became open on the court, he nominated Sandra Day O'Connor to the Court. She was approved as many women applauded.

On March 30, 1981, some two months after his inauguration, President Reagan spoke to union delegates at a Washington hotel. He left the hotel and walked toward his limousine. A small crowd had gathered, among them a tall, broad-shouldered young man who carried a gun. The young man lifted the gun, pointed it at the President, and pulled the trigger. A bullet streaked by Mike Deaver's shoulder and whizzed toward the President's heart.

The President

The .22 caliber bullet zipped by Deaver. It struck the armor-plated limousine, then flattened out like a dime. It riccocheted off the armor plating and slammed into the left side of the President's chest, inches from his heart.

The President heard loud cracks. "It was like firecrackers going off," said one spectator. The crazed gunman, John Hinckley, fired six times. His bullets hit the President, a secret service agent, a cop and Ron's press secretary, the heavy-set, balding James Brady. Police and agents buried Hinckley under an avalanche of bodies. They took him off to a mental hospital, where he would remain for the rest of his life.

Ron didn't know he had been wounded. Jerry Parr, one of his bodyguards, pushed him into the back of the limousine to escape the hail of bullets. The President fell hard on the floor and felt a sharp pain.

"Take off!" Parr shouted at the driver.

"You broke my ribs," Ron growled, the pain now intense. Parr fanned his hands across the President's chest. He felt no blood.

Then he saw blood gush from the President's mouth. Parr thought: Maybe I did break one of the President's ribs. He told the driver to speed to nearby George Washington Hospital.

The President walked into the hospital's emergency room,

his face white. His knees began to sag. Nurses put him on a table and rolled him into surgery.

Doctors pulled off his blood-soaked blue jacket. They saw where the bullet had entered near his left arm pit. It had stopped within a finger tip of his heart. The surgeons knew they had to get that bullet out quickly—before it moved.

Nancy arrived. Deaver met her. "He's taken a bullet," Deaver said. "But he's all right."

Deaver took her to the President. She put her hand on her husband's forehead. He looked up, face still white. He smiled and said, "Honey, I forgot to duck."

Surgeons told Ron that they were ready to try to take out the bullet. "Please tell me," Ron said with a faint smile, "you are really all Republicans."

Minutes later a surgeon probed a finger into the chest of the unconscious President. He felt the bullet and tugged it out.

Several hours later the President awoke. He wanted to know who else had been hurt. He was told that two of the three wounded men would be all right—but that press secretary Brady might die. Ron told Nancy that he felt bad that someone would die because of a bullet meant for him. Brady survived, though crippled for life. Ron ordered that no one else would hold the title of press secretary while he was President—and no one did.

Two weeks later Ron sat behind his huge oak desk in the Oval Office. He and his aides begun to plan to reach Ron's three main goals. One: "To get the government off the back of people" by spending less money on health, education, welfare, the environment, low-cost housing and other social programs. Two: He wanted to cut income taxes. Three: He wanted to build more muscle into the United States military arm so that it could strike back at terrorists in the Middle East while also keeping the nation safe from a nuclear attack.

He had appointed a cabinet to help reach those goals. His old California friend, Caspar Weinberger, headed the Defense Department. Alexander Haig, a former general and Nixon aide, was Secretary of State, setting foreign policy. Donald Regan, a Wall Street broker, took charge of the Treasury. Ron told Regan to balance the budget. What the Treasury took in from taxes, Ron had promised voters, would balance what the government spent.

But the one closest to the President was Nancy. If Nancy thought an aide lazy, incompetent, or disloyal, she whispered in Deaver's ear. And that man or woman vanished from the White House. With a regal walk, a smile frozen on her face, she stayed aloof from White House aides, Deaver excepted. Behind her back, some staffers called her Queen Nancy.

She could not sleep well for weeks after the attack on Ron. Her wafer-thin figure turned even slimmer, her dress size shrinking from a size 6 to a size 4. She began to call a California astrologer she knew. Astrologers believe that the stars can tell us what will happen, good or bad, on a given day or week. She asked the astrologer what were "safe" days for Ron to travel. Aides grumbled that a fortune teller was telling the President of the United States where and when to travel.

Ron and Nancy lived and slept in the historic, exquisitely decorated rooms above the Oval Office. Ron reminded old friends that he had been born in a room above a store in Tampico. Grinning, he said, "I'm still living above the store."

Ron slept until 7:30 most mornings. He and Nancy ate breakfast together in the family's dining room. Then he took an elevator one floor down to the Oval Office. He met with Meese, Deaver and Baker to discuss the day's schedule. A National Security adviser briefed him on secrets picked up by United States Intelligence during the past twelve hours. Vice President Bush dropped in to talk about foreign policy. He knew what went on in foreign nations, having been Chief of United States Intelligence. Ron had no experience in foreign relations. He came to depend on Bush to teach him what he had to know.

Mornings were also filled by talks with visitors—kings, princes, archbishops, businessmen, labor-union leaders. At noon he lunched in his office with Bush or Chief of Staff Baker. Ron usually ordered an old favorite, macaroni and cheese, or a small steak, plus a dessert, often fruit in syrup.

Papers flowed across his desk for him to read all during the day. President Reagan insisted that his aides boil down even

The President and Nancy present an award to Michael Jackson for his contributions to American music. To the amusement of his children, Ron's favorite music was the big-band swing sounds of the 1940s. "That," he would tell Michael, drumming his fingers to Glenn Miller's *In the Mood*, "is real music."
COURTESY REAGAN PRESIDENTIAL MATERIALS STAFF

the most complicated arguments into one-page memos. Ron read each memo carefully. At the bottom of the page he checked off one of four boxes:

Approved

Approved as Amended by the President

Rejected

No Action (which meant further review of the problem by his aides).

Jimmy Carter had been called "a slave to detail." Carter even kept lists showing who was playing and when on the White House tennis courts. Reagan left details for aides to puzzle out while he spent his time deciding long-range goals.

Ron ate dinner alone with Nancy in their upstairs family quarters. The twenty-five rooms were shared by the Reagans, their servants, and occasional guests, including their four children and their families. The upstairs White House had been redesigned by Nancy. The colors were pink, salmon and yellow. The cost, almost a million dollars, was paid by friends of the Reagans.

Both Ron and Nancy had exercise rooms. Nancy rode a stationary bike. Ron chinned on horizontal bars. His son Mike gaped incredulously one day as his seventy-four-year-old father did ten chin ups that Mike, half his age, would not dare. Ron told friends that the exercising had added almost two inches to his chest.

The Carter White House had been austere: dinners were simple meat-and-potato kind of affairs. The Reagans brought back the pomp and glitter of White House parties that John and Jackie Kennedy had favored. Guests included stars like Cary Grant, Bob Hope, Frank Sinatra, what Ron often called "the old Hollywood crowd." Guests sipped cocktails and champagne

At work in the Oval Office, the President goes over papers for his approval or disapproval. Newspaperman Lou Cannon watched Reagan as a governor and as a president. Cannon wrote of Reagan as a chief executive: "He learns by trial and error, acting in a way which worked before . . . While he has a passive nature, he persists to reach the goals he has set for himself."
COURTESY REAGAN PRESIDENTIAL MATERIALS STAFF

while strolling violinists played. The women wore jewels and long flowing gowns, the men in tuxedos. Maids and butlers served pheasant and other delicacies.

The poor and homeless in America's cities, meanwhile, had swelled to the hundreds of thousands. Families lived on welfare checks that didn't add up in a year to the cost of one of Nancy's glittering gowns. Critics wrote that the Reagans lived a life of luxury on the taxpayers' money while less of that tax money now went to the poor.

On weekends Nancy and Ron climbed into their helicopter and flew to Camp David, a hideaway in the nearby Maryland mountains. At Camp David, Ron golfed, hiked and fished for a trout.

But the President's favorite place was the "heavenly ranch" high in the hills above Santa Barbara. Every few months he and Nancy flew west for a vacation of two weeks to a month. His four children and the grandchildren came to the ranch for week-long stays. Nancy preferred the luxury of their Pacific Palisades home. But she stayed with Ron because she knew how life on the ranch invigorated him.

The President rode his favorite horse, Little Man, a thorough-bred he had raised from a colt. Ron fed the ranch's other horses. He changed their shoes and cleaned out the barns. His muscled arms chopped wood for the house's only heat—two stone fire-places. He played with his dog, Fuzzy, a German shepherd. Fuzzy was crippled by arthritis. A doctor told the President: "We'll have to put Fuzzy to sleep or he'll be in terrible pain."

The President fed Fuzzy a last meal of his favorite tid-bits, then gave him to the doctor. Later he dug a grave in a nearby hill. He covered the grave with stones so the coyotes and bears that prowled the hills would not dig up Fuzzy.

Back in Washington, Democrats and Republicans in Congress joined to pass legislation that Ron had promised: a tax cut. He reduced the money that had been going to agencies to fight Lyndon Johnson's war on poverty.

His Department of Interior chief, James Watt, tried to open up more federal-owned land to mining and lumbering companies, which stripped the land, digging up minerals like coal and cutting down trees. Conservationists roared that Watt was giving away natural resources. Watt later quit. A new Interior chief became tougher on the mining and lumbering companies.

Ron loved nature, the wilderness, the scenic and unspoiled beauty of places like Camp David and his ranch. But he thought that environmentalists had to be aware that trees had to be cut down for wood, mines had to be dug for minerals like coal. What infuriated environmentalists was his seeming indifference to rivers and harbors polluted by big companies that dumped waste material. And he refused to take action to prevent "acid rain"—chemicals from factory smokestacks mixing with rain—that ruined forests.

The President poured money into the Defense Department. He wanted more nuclear weapons and rockets aimed at the heart of Russia—the nation he had called that "evil empire." He fell in love with a science-fiction-like system that would act like an umbrella to fend off Soviet missiles as they rained down on the United States. The system was called Strategic Defense Initiative, or S.D.I. The idea of invisible beams knocking down missiles reminded reporters of the movie *Star Wars*.

Star Wars, as it would be called, angered the Russians. S.D.I., said the Soviets, was a system aimed at destroying Russia. Ron said no, the system was a defensive one. But, he told aides, if the Russians were scared of S.D.I., he liked the plan even better. He ordered millions to be spent to perfect S.D.I.

By late 1982, the United States looked a lot healthier. The stock market spurted upward, its Dow Jones average shooting from below 1,000 to 1,500 and then soaring above 2,000. Unemployment sunk to its lowest level in years—only about five percent of Americans were out of work, down from nearly nine percent in the Carter years. Homes tripled in value. And inflation dropped from about eighteen percent in the Carter years to below eight percent. Stag-flation was gone, prosperous times were here again.

"Reaganomics is a word I don't hear so often from my critics," the President told reporters in 1983. "Maybe that means Reaganomics is working."

Four Presidents: Ronald Reagan, Gerald Ford, Jimmy Carter and Richard Nixon. President Reagan often called Nixon for advice on foreign affairs, especially on China, where Nixon had visited as President. But President Reagan was not known ever to have called Carter. Both men had a dislike for each other that went beyond their differences in politics.
COURTESY REAGAN PRESIDENTIAL MATERIALS STAFF

But liberals said, "Whoah! Let's take another look at this economy. The poor and homeless are growing in numbers every day. The number of unemployed minorities is still near an all-time high. We are not spending enough money to cure drug addiction. The number of addicts and the crime rate are both soaring. This is not a healthy nation."

And Reagan's tax cuts meant that the nation was taking in less money than it was spending. In 1980, the Carter administration spent $60 billion more than it took in. Reagan had promised to balance the budget, matching spending with income. But by 1984, the government was spending $175 billion more than the treasury took in. Ron blamed the Democrats in Congress for the deficit gap. "If they let me veto some of those big spending bills," he said, "we will have a balanced budget."

The U.S. government owed about $1 trillion in 1980. In 1985, it owed almost $2.5 trillion. The treasury had to pay huge sums in interest to people who loaned the government money by buying bonds. Those billions of dollars in interest each year, said liberals, could buy food for the poor.

But by 1984, most Americans felt better about themselves and their country. And even liberals genuinely liked the affable President. "I think he's a terrible President," said House Speaker Tip O'Neill, a Democrat. "But he would have made a great king."

The President smiled cheerfully each morning to White House servants. He had a quick and fiery temper, as he had showed in Nashua to George Bush. Yet he rarely lost his temper with a servant or a secretary. But people as close to him as Mike Deaver sensed that Ron kept most people an arm's length away from his inner self. That inner self was off-limits to everyone and reserved only to Nancy and on occasion his children.

For years his son Mike had wrestled with a secret shame. When he was eight, Mike had been sexually molested by a camp counselor. Confused, Mike didn't tell Jane or Ron because he thought he—and not the counselor—had done something bad. That incident tortured Mike for more than thirty years. He feared that his mother and dad might blame him.

Finally he went to a psychiatrist who told him, "Tell your father."

Mike drove to the Santa Barbara ranch. His wife took Ron's grandchild, Cameron, for a walk. He, Nancy and Ron walked around the corral. Mike said he had something terrible to tell them. He burst into tears.

"Tell us," Nancy said softly, her arms around Mike.

"I was molested by a camp counselor . . ." He blurted out the words that had been locked inside him for thirty years, then couldn't go on. Tears flowed down his flushed face.

Ron's face showed shock. "Why didn't you tell me about this when it happened?"

"Because I was afraid you would stop liking me."

"You should have known better," his father said. Mike nodded, knowing his father was right.

But such heart-to-heart talks were rare between Ron and his children. Mike thought he seemed too much in love with Nancy to have any room left over in his emotions for his kids.

The Secret Service guarded Mike and the other Reagan children and their families. Because of a misunderstanding, the Secret Service accused Mike of being a kleptomaniac—someone who steals because of a mental illness. At first Ron believed the Secret Service. Mike had to bring Ron's minister to his father to convince the President that the Secret Service was wrong.

"I'm sorry," Ron said to Mike. "I guess it was all a misunderstanding." Telling of the incident in his book, On the Outside Looking In, Mike added: "I struggled to tell my father that I loved him. Instead I could only say, 'You know, you've never told me that you love me.' "

Ron blinked at his son, surprised. Then he said, "Michael, I love you."

In his book Mike Reagan told two stories that gave a glimpse into the world Ron Reagan reserved mostly for Nancy and his kids. Once the President was showing Mike and his two grandchildren the Oval Office. A White House guide led a line of tourists into the office. He saw the President, shooed the gaping tourists out, apologizing as he left.

"What he didn't realize," wrote Mike, "was that dad likes people and he wouldn't have minded talking to visitors."

Mike brought his children's twenty-one-year-old baby sitter, Dorothy, to the White House. An outspoken liberal, Dorothy opposed the President's cutting of funds to aid the physically and mentally handicapped. As she posed with the President for a photo, she told him she was a Democrat.

The President placed an arm around Dorothy and said, "When I was a child, I used to speak as a child, think as a child, reason as a child. When I became a man, I did away with childish things. I think that's first Corinthians, 13:11."

Dorothy, a religious person, was impressed that the President knew his Bible so well. And she laughed politely at the President's joke: that only those with childish minds could be Democrats.

The next night Ron saw Dorothy walking with his granddaughter in a White House corridor. To her amazement, she saw the President hurry over to her. He asked her to walk with him in the Rose Garden. He told her that he was sorry for having quoted scripture to her.

"I shouldn't have done that, and it has bothered me ever since," the President said. "You should feel free to be a Democrat or Republican or Independent and vote for whomever you want. I hope you will accept my apology."

Dorothy told Mike what the President had said to her. "I can no longer believe," she told Mike, "that this man would knowingly hurt anybody. He's wonderful."

"You're right," Mike told her.

Early in 1984, Ron asked Nancy: Should he run for a second term? He would be seventy-three years old in November—the oldest President in history. Nancy said the decision was up to him.

But she added: "If you do run, I hope that in your second term you can bring us closer to world peace."

Ron decided to run. In Moscow there was a man, rising rapidly to power, who would sit down with the man from Dixon, Illinois, to try to make Nancy's hope a reality.

The Peace Maker

"Now, Mermie," said the President, and Maureen Reagan knew she was in trouble with her father. He always called her Mermie when he was going to disagree with her.

Maureen had come to Oval Office on this summer's day in 1984 to plead with her father to support a new amendment being proposed for the United States Constitution. The Equal Rights Amendment (ERA) would guarantee equal rights for women. A company would break the law if it paid a man more than it paid a woman for doing the same job.

Maureen now worked for the Republican National Committee in Washington. The Committee was organizing the campaign to re-elect President Reagan and Vice President Bush. The Democrats had nominated former Vice President Walter Mondale to run for President. And they had picked Congresswoman Geraldine Ferraro to run for Vice President—the first time a woman had been nominated to run for Vice President.

Maureen told her father that women seemed to prefer the Mondale-Ferraro ticket. "Support ERA," Maureen told her father, "and more women will vote for you."

The President shook his head. "Mermie," he said, "what we really have here is another way for government to interfere with people's lives." He had run for office promising to get govern-

117

ment out of people's lives. "If ERA passes," he said, "women will share the duties of men, including combat as soldiers and sailors. I don't want to live in a country where women are drafted into combat."

Maureen went away feeling glum. She knew that more women had been appointed to Reagan's cabinet, than to any other cabinet in history. And he was the first to name a woman to the Supreme Court. But like millions of other women, Maureen disagreed with him on ERA, which was defeated.

Other women disagreed with him on abortion. The President had opposed any use of taxpayers' money to provide free abortions.

But most Americans—men and women, Democrats and Republicans—thought the nation was a better place to live than in 1980. Reagan and Bush were swept back into office aboard a tidal wave of votes. The Republicans won forty-eight of the fifty states.

As he began his second term, the President had to surround himself with new aides. Ed Meese had become the nation's attorney general, heading the Justice Department. Mike Deaver left government to start a business advising companies that wanted to do business with government agencies.

The third member of Reagan's trio, Chief of Staff James Baker, had become weary of saying no to the hundreds of people who wanted to see the President each day. He switched jobs with Donald Regan. Baker became Secretary of the Treasury and Regan became Chief of Staff.

Regan was a burly, quick-tempered ex-Marine who cracked his thick fists on his desk when angry. He had run a big Wall Street firm where everyone knew he was "The Boss." Maureen disliked him and called him "The Dictator." But the President liked someone close to him who could iron out the small problems while the President wrestled with the big ones.

Reagan and Regan kidded each other about how close their names were. The President once told Regan: "You know, I've been told that the smart Irish called themselves Ray-gun. The dumb ones took the name Ree-gan."

As 1985 began, Americans were riding a wave of prosperity that had lasted three years. Pay envelopes were fatter and the stock market hit an alltime high. In 1986, the President signed the Tax Reform Act which cut taxes for most Americans. But

Nancy and Ron dance a few steps at a party celebrating the second inaugural in 1985. Behind them is a swing band playing one of the President's favorites from the 1940s. The inaugural parties cost millions of dollars, setting off angry blasts from Reagan critics that he threw away money while cutting off money to the poor.
COURTESY REAGAN PRESIDENTIAL MATERIALS STAFF

the government still spent more than it took in. The United States Treasury owed trillions of dollars—and that debt jumped hourly by millions of dollars. To balance the budget, which Reagan promised to do but never did, he and the Congress agreed on the Gramm-Rudman law. That law made future administrations spend no more each year than they took in.

Growing challenges to the President included the swelling army of homeless men, women and children sleeping in the streets, and the millions of others who bought and sold illegal drugs despite a campaign led by Nancy to "Say No to Drugs." The police said most crimes were committed by people who bought or sold drugs. Farmers in the midwest protested that they paid more for farm machines but got lower prices for their meat, fruit and vegetables. Middle East terrorists frightened Americans, many of whom cancelled vacations in Europe. Arab terrorists captured six Americans and held them as hostages in Lebanon. The terrorists were sending a message to the President: Stop your support of Israel. The Israelis were battling Arabs who wanted their own Palestinian state.

The President tried to comfort relatives of the hostages. They begged him: Can't you free the hostages? When the relatives left his office, the President's face was drawn taut and lined with worry. He had to free the hostages, he told Regan. But how?

The President's new National Security Adviser was Robert "Bud" McFarlane, a wiry, tight-lipped ex-Marine. He heard that the Iran government, which had captured and later released American hostages in 1980, needed anti-aircraft rockets for its war against neighboring Iraq. An Iranian official told McFarlane: Give us anti-aircraft rockets and we'll see to it that the hostages in Lebanon are freed.

McFarlane told the President that thirty million dollars worth of rockets would be a small price to pay for the hostages. The President told McFarlane to try to make the swap.

Guns roared, meanwhile, in Central America, where a rebel army in Nicaragua fought to overthrow the government. President Reagan argued that the government was led by Communists.

Reagan wanted to send aid to the rebels, who were called Contras. But Democrats and Republicans argued against it. They said the government had been elected by the people of Nicaragua, so they passed a law prohibiting aid to the Contras.

McFarlane sold the weapons to the Iranians for thirty million dollars. But at the last minute the Iranians said they would not help free the hostages. A little later McFarlane quit as Security Adviser. John Poindexter, a quiet-spoken, pipe-smoking admiral, succeeded him. One of his top aides was Oliver North, a Marine colonel. Poindexter and North decided to secretly ship some of that thirty million dollars to the Contras in Nicaragua, even though aid to the Contras was illegal.

By 1985, many Americans had become fascinated by the new ruler of Soviet Russia. He was the Communist Party's General Secretary, the balding, plump Mikhail Gorbachev. In his mid-50s, he was much younger than the men who had ruled Russia with iron fists for the past fifty years. He had grown up amid the poverty of Russia. He knew that men and women waited in long lines each day to buy food for their supper, usually tiny hunks of horsemeat. They shivered in smelly, cramped rooms. Not one Russian in a thousand owned a car or a washing machine. Only the privileged few Communist bosses owned a color-TV set.

Gorbachev knew that millions of Russians were getting unsettling news from others who visited western Europe and America. The Russian people now knew that the ordinary man in Europe and America enjoyed luxuries that Russians could only dream of. How long, Gorbachev worried, would his people live in poverty before they rose up and overthrew Communism?

Gorbachev also knew that his government was spending billions of rubles to build up its army, navy and nuclear weapons. If that money could be spent to build cars, washing machines and TV sets, his people would be happier.

In Washington, meanwhile, President Reagan was telling the world that his Strategic Defense Initiative—what the newspapers called Star Wars—would knock nuclear rockets out of space. If it worked, Star Wars would make both America and the world safe from nuclear attack.

But look at the cost, critics screamed. Yes, said the President,

Star Wars will cost billions. But making a nation safe is worth any cost.

Gorbachev protested that Star Wars was aimed at destroying Soviet Russia. President Reagan knew that Gorbachev could not afford to build a Star Wars system. Its cost would break the backs of the Soviet people. But if America's Star Wars worked, Russia's costly rockets would be worthless.

The President smiled knowingly when he got a message from Gorbachev late in 1985. Gorbachev wanted to talk about reducing the number of nuclear warheads aimed at each country's heart. The two agreed to meet in Geneva, Switzerland, late in 1985.

Thousands of reporters and photographers and hundreds of TV cameras watched as the two leaders shook hands. They liked each other right away. As their hundreds of assistants conferred, the President turned to the General Secretary and said, "Let's get some fresh air and have a meeting alone."

They walked to a nearby lakeside cottage. For more than a half hour they talked, alone except for their two interpreters. Gorbachev could speak English, but the President knew no Russian.

"This is a unique situation," the President told Gorbachev. "Here we are, two men in a room together. We're the only two in the world who could bring about World War III. At the same time, maybe we're the only two who could bring about world peace. Maybe we can get together and get rid of the things that make us not trust each other."

The President said he was an optimist—one who believes things will get better. He told a story about an optimist. There was a boy, he said, who was given a room filled with horse manure as a birthday present. The boy grabbed a shovel and began to dig, saying to his parents: "There must be a pony in here somewhere!"

Gorbachev laughed at the story. Then the President made an offer: He would share the secrets of Star Wars with the Russians. Both sides might be safe against a nuclear attack.

"No," snapped Gorbachev. The only answer was to ban all nuclear weapons.

Gorbachev and his pretty wife, Raisa, invited Nancy and the President to dinner. Raisa was a professor at a Moscow university. She talked knowingly about world history, annoying Nancy who could get in only a word or two. After dinner, Nancy turned to Don Regan and said, "Who does that dame think she is, anyway?"

At dinner the Gorbachevs asked the President what it was like to be a Hollywood star. The former actor talked of the glamorous people he had known—the dashing Errol Flynn, the breezy Bette Davis, the ravishing Marilyn Monroe, the tough Humphrey Bogart. The Gorbachevs sat spellbound as the old actor weaved story after story.

The two leaders agreed to meet again at a second "Summit" meeting. Eleven months later, in the fall of 1986, they met in Reykjavik, Iceland. Again their hundreds of aides talked about the details of a treaty that would reduce the number of nuclear weapons.

"Those are the small problems," the President told his Chief of Staff. "They're often harder to solve than the big problems. But once you solve the big problems, the little ones disappear."

After two days of trying to solve little and big problems, the two men still could not agree on how to reduce their piles of weapons. Suddenly the President turned to Gorbachev and asked, "You talk about 'elimination of all strategic forces.' What does that mean?"

"I meant I would favor eliminating all nuclear weapons."

"All nuclear weapons. Well, Mikhail, that's exactly what I've been talking about all along. That's what we have long wanted to do—get rid of all nuclear weapons. That's always been my goal."

"Then why don't we agree on it?" Gorbachev asked.

"We should. That's what I've been trying to tell you," the President said.

Gorbachev hesitated. Before he would agree to a ban on nuclear weapons, he said, America had to give up testing Star Wars.

The President could not give up Star Wars. That weapon, he

believed, had brought Gorbachev here to talk about no more nuclear weapons.

The President said no. Stiffly, the two men said goodbye. As they shook hands in the frosty Iceland air, Gorbachev asked the President: Would he change his mind? The President said no, he would not.

That night the gloomy President flew home. He turned to Don Regan, placed his thumb and forefinger an inch apart and said, "We were that close" to agreeing on peace.

Had the President lost his last chance for world peace?

The Hero

The President walked into the White House office. He tossed a baseball up into the air, then caught it with one hand. General Secretary Gorbachev watched the President toss the baseball, which the President had just signed for his friend, Hall of Fame baseball player Joe DiMaggio. DiMaggio had asked the President if Gorbachev would also sign the baseball.

The President smiled at Gorbachev on this day late in 1987. Gorbachev had just arrived in Washington for a third Summit.

"Well," said the President, still tossing the baseball, which Gorbachev later signed, "are we going to play ball?"

Gorbachev had to smile. Yes, he had come to Washington—as the Americans say—to play ball. And he knew he had thrown his hardest pitch at Reykjavik in Iceland—and lost. The President would keep on testing Star Wars. If Gorbachev wanted to stop pouring money into weapons, he'd have to live with Star Wars.

"Mr. President," Gorbachev told Reagan, "do what you think you have to do (with Star Wars). If, in the end, you want to deploy it (Star Wars weapons), go ahead and deploy. Who am I to tell you what to do? I think you are wasting money, but if that's what you want to do, go ahead."

The two leaders agreed to sign a treaty that would destroy

more than 2,000 missiles on both sides. No longer would America and its allies aim intermediate-range missiles at Russia from western Europe. And no longer would Russia aim intermediate-range missiles at Europe.

Gorbachev and the President also agreed to start work on a treaty that would destroy all long-range nuclear missiles, those aimed at Russia from the U.S., and those aimed at the United States from Russia. The President knew that START, as that treaty was called, wouldn't be signed for years. But he told Gorbachev, "I think we trust each other more." And he added, "We have lit the sky with hope for all people of goodwill."

Some six months later, in June of 1988, the President flew to Moscow to officially sign the treaty banning intermediate missiles. While there he talked to writers, artists, religious people and others who were called dissidents, who spoke out against the harshness of Communist rule.

The President praised Gorbachev for making that rule less harsh. He applauded Gorbachev's policies of "glasnot"—more freedom and openness—and "perestroika", the removal of strict government rules. But he made clear to the dissidents that Russia was still a police state.

"I didn't want to kick anybody in the shins," the President said later, referring to Gorbachev. Reagan believed that Gorbachev had been good for Russia and world peace. But the old anti-Communist fighter would never take back what he had once said—that this had been "an evil empire."

The four Gorbachev-Reagan Summits began to melt the Cold War that had kept the two superpowers a glacier apart for forty years. "If we have made war more distant," Reagan told Gorbachev as he left Moscow, "then that is a source of satisfaction."

Gorbachev began to talk to leaders in the United States, France and England. He wanted to spend Russian money that formerly went for nuclear bombs on things the Russian people wanted—cars, computers, farm machinery, Coca Cola—things that would ease their lives and make them happy. As the 1990s began, the symbol of the barrier between East and West—the Berlin Wall—had been torn down. The winds of democracy

General Secretary Gorbachev holds a Russian child in Red Square and tells him, "Give grandfather Reagan a kiss." The President kissed the boy, one more sign of the warming up of relations between cold war foes. At right in the rear can be seen the cap of a United States Naval officer. He is probably the one who must always be within a few feet of the President and carrying the "black box." The box would put the Commander-in-Chief in touch with his generals if America were suddenly attacked.
COURTESY REAGAN PRESIDENTIAL MATERIALS STAFF

swept through a shattered Iron Curtain. Communist countries—Czechoslovakia, Poland, and East Germany among them—had begun free elections. The "evil empire" was swiftly turning into nations where people enjoyed—for the first time in their lives—freedom and prosperity.

The four Summits had made Ronald Reagan the leader of the western democracies. But at home he seemed at times to be a confused man trying to put together a jigsaw puzzle he didn't understand. The Iran-Contra affair had exploded in his face, sending shock waves that seemed strong enough to blow him out of the Oval Office as a disgraced President.

The scandal began with news that America had sold weapons to Iran, the dictatorship that had once held Americans hostage. Then came news that the Iranians' thirty million dollars was supposed to be diverted to the Contras, which was illegal. And one day Ed Meese, the Attorney General, told a white-faced President that most of the thirty million dollars had never reached the Contras. At least twenty million dollars had vanished.

Appearing on television, the President told the nation that we had not swapped weapons for hostages. No one believed him, not even Nancy, who told her husband that the newspaper stories clearly showed he wasn't telling the truth. Then the President said that maybe he had agreed to swap weapons for hostages—he didn't remember. Finally, months later, he confessed there had been an attempt to swap rockets for hostages. America had been double-crossed by the Iranians, he admitted, and the whole thing was a blunder.

Washington talked of a second President resigning in the mist of a scandal. Reagan ordered a high-level panel, headed by respected former Texas Senator John Tower, to look into the Iran-Contra affair. The Tower committee concluded that the President had not known of the illegal diversion of funds to the Contras. But it blamed Chief of Staff Don Regan for letting men like Admiral Poindexter and Colonel North run an illegal operation right under the nose of the President. Don Regan knew nothing about the money going to the Contras, said the Tower committee, but he *should* have known about it.

President Reagan hated to fire people—and rarely did. But Nancy growled that Regan had to go. "There was tension between Ronnie and me about Regan," Nancy later admitted. Finally, without meeting Regan face to face, the President put former Senator Howard Baker in his place. A bitter Regan

The President, his Vice President and cabinet officers: Vice President George Bush stands next to the President. Caspar Weinberger is on the far left. Next to him is former Chief of Staff James Baker. On Baker's left is Secretary of State George Schultz. On his left is Ed Meese and on Meese's left is Transportation Secretary Elizabeth Dole. Nancy once asked Bush to tell Ron to fire Don Regan. Bush said, "That's not my role." Nancy snapped, "That is exactly your role."
COURTESY REAGAN PRESIDENTIAL MATERIALS STAFF

stalked out of the White House, refusing even to speak to the man he had served loyally for six years.

More than a half-dozen top officials, Bud McFarlane and Colonel North among them, stood trial for the Iran-Contra affair, McFarlane and North were among those found guilty. Before his trial Poindexter demanded that President Reagan testify and produce pages of his diary. The diary would show, Poindexter said, that the President knew about the money going to the Contras—a charge President Reagan had always denied.

Other scandals made the President wince during his last year and a half in the White House. He and the Congress shared the blame for not watching closely how hundreds of savings and loan banks were being operated. Cheating bankers plundered those S & Ls at a cost to taxpayers of several billion dollars. And federal housing officials were caught steering money into their pockets—money that was supposed to house the poor.

Among those tripped up by scandals were Mike Deaver and Ed Meese, two of the men closest to the President. Deaver was accused of using his White House influence to get contracts for clients. Meese sat for days on a witness stand during a trial about a New York City housing scandal—but he escaped being charged with doing anything wrong. More than one hundred top Reagan officials were accused in a variety of scandals.

That was the bad news during the President's last days in office. Good news came from his children. All four had once made him frown when they told reporters he was a distant father. His oldest, Maureen, talked about becoming a leader in feminist movements. Mike had purged his inner torment and was a happy salesman and father of two. Ron, Jr., the youngest, had etched new worry lines on his father's face by telling reporters he would become a ballet dancer. To the President, ballet dancers were sissies at best, gay men at worst. But his old movie-star pal, tap dancer Gene Kelly, told the President that lots of ballet dancers were he-men. Ron later became a journalist and a father.

But Patti Davis, Ron and Nancy's daughter, remained a rebellious liberal. She wrote two novels, one featuring a crafty governor of California and his ambitious wife, the other featuring a bumbling President of the United States and his nasty wife. Her brother Mike scolded her for "trashing" the family. "My biggest failure in life," Nancy once said, "was my failure to mend our relationship with Patti."

As the President's popularity soared in the 1980s, so did the career of his first wife, Jane Wyman. She came out of retirement to become one of the stars of television's *Falcon Crest.*

In November of 1988 Vice President Bush was elected President with his running mate, Indiana Senator Dan Quayle. As President Reagan congratulated his successor, he made clear he was happy to be leaving the White House.

"It's very fine living," he told people. "But every once in a while you do look out the window and see people walking by and you say to yourself, 'There's something they can do and I

In retirement, the former President wears ranch-style clothes for cutting wood, riding horses and fixing fences. Closing in on eighty, he had a physique envied by men fifty years younger. But once a President, always a President. He told a friend in 1989, "When I hear a news announcer say, 'The President today decided . . .' I turn and hear myself asking, 'What did I decide today?' "
COURTESY REAGAN PRESIDENTIAL MATERIALS STAFF

can't do.' I can't just walk down to the corner drugstore and pick up a birthday card or a magazine or something."

In January of 1989 he flew back to his home in Pacific Palisades and his ranch in the hills above Santa Barbara. He rode his horses, cut brushes, chopped wood, and wrote his memoirs.

Historians talked about how the Reagan Revolution had changed United States government. From 1982 to 1988, he had added thirty percent more employees to the Justice Department, twenty-three percent more to Treasury, eleven percent more to the Environmental Protection Agency, eleven percent to the State Department, and eight percent to the Department of Defense.

He had shrunk the Department of Education by thirty-one percent, the Department for low-cost housing by seventeen percent, the Labor Department by fifteen percent, the Department of Energy by thirteen percent, and the Space Agency (NASA) by almost two percent. By one estimate, funding for the poor during the Reagan years was cut by $57 billion.

Others called these changes in the shape of the government a "counter-revolution." President Reagan always claimed that he was for helping the poor, the sick, the aged, as well as minorities in big-city ghettos. But he thought that the pendulum of social-welfare programs had swung too far. Liberals, he said, wasted money because they thought that money alone would solve problems of poverty. As he often said, paraphrasing his idol, FDR, "the best poverty program is a job." In the Reagan counter-revolution, he wanted to swing the pendulum back toward the New Deal idea that welfare helps those who *can't* work, and that jobs help those who *can* work.

In late 1989, former President Reagan chatted with young people in a Manhattan home for troubled teenagers. "Why doesn't the government spend more money on the homeless than on nuclear weapons?" asked a sixteen year old.

The former President talked about how he had to build up a weakened army, navy and air force. "And now," he said, "we are closer to peace with the Soviet Union than in forty years." He looked at the kids, many former drug addicts, and said, "There must have been times when you wondered if anyone cared. Yes! People do care. I care about you, and that's why I am here."

He described how poor the Reagans had been back in Dixon and how his father had been an alcoholic. "There were nights when I was angry and frustrated and wondered, 'Why?' " Then he told them how his mother's optimism had helped him over those bad times. "She told us that 'something good will happen, and you'll realize it was for the best.' "

He told the kids how bad he had felt when he failed to get the job at Montgomery Ward after graduating from college. They laughed when he said, "If I'd gotten that first job, I might still be working at Montgomery Ward."

This was the essence of the Reagan message: A person had to stand on his or her own two feet. A person can't always depend on welfare or on the government—and certainly not on drugs—to help them over the rough times. Like the nineteenth century pioneers who were Dutch Reagan's grandparents and his role models, individuals have to go out on their own and be self-reliant. Self-reliance was a nineteenth century quality badly needed, he argued, for both the twentieth and twenty-first centuries.

Most liberals disagreed, claiming that twentieth century America had changed too much for anyone to be self-reliant. But millions would enshrine Ronald Reagan in the same way that Americans had enshrined Franklin D. Roosevelt and John F. Kennedy—symbols of both change and hope.

A friend once scolded Nancy Reagan for looking at Ron with her idolizing gaze. "Why do you look at him that way?" the friend said. "It's as if you were saying, 'He's my hero.' "

"But he is my hero," Nancy said.

He was a hero for more than fifty years to millions of others who gazed at him adoringly as a movie star, a TV personality, a governor, a president, and a world leader for peace.

For the teenage lifeguard back on the Rock River in Illinois who lived in a world of pretend and dreamed that one day he would be the hero who runs a hundred yards for a touchdown, the run was done and much more than a touchdown scored.

For Further Reading

There are a number of books I would suggest to people who want to know more about Ronald Reagan. They would include:

Early Reagan, the Rise to Power, by Anne Edwards (William Morrow, 1987). Ms. Edwards details, more than any other biographer, the young years of Reagan from Tampico, Illinois, to the governorship of California.

Ronald Reagan, by Lou Cannon (Putnam, 1982). A California and Washington newspaperman, Cannon wrote about Reagan both as a governor and president.

Ronald Reagan, by George Sullivan (Julian Messner, 1985).

Mister President, The Story of Ronald Reagan, by Mary Virginia Fox (Enslow, 1985).

Ronald Reagan, His Life Story in Pictures, by Stanley P. Friedman. (Dodd, Mead, 1986).

On the Outside Looking In, by Michael Reagan with Joe Hyams (Zebra Books, 1988).

The Acting President, by Bob Schieffer and Gary Paul Gates (E.P. Dutton, 1989).

First Father, First Daughter, by Maureen Reagan (Little Brown, 1989).

For the Record, by Don Regan (Harcourt Brace Jovanovich, 1988).

Where's the Rest of Me, by Ronald Reagan and Richard G. Hoobler (Carz, 1981; Duell, Sloan & Pearce, 1965).

Index